D0667152

yes,

There Is Something You Can Do

yes,

There Is Something You Can Do

150 Prayers, Poems, and Meditations for Times of Need

JAMIE C. MILLER

FAIR WINDS
PRESS
GLOUCESTER, MASSACHUSETTS

© 2003 by Fair Winds Press

All rights reserved. No part of this book may be reproduced in any form or by any means, electronic or mechanical, without prior permission in writing from the publisher.

First published in the U.S.A. by
Fair Winds Press
33 Commercial Street
Gloucester, Massachusetts 01930-5089

Library of Congress Cataloging-in-Publication Data Available

ISBN: 1-931412-33-2

10 9 8 7 6 5 4 3 2 1

Cover design by Yee Design
Cover image by Gettyimages™
Design by Yee Design

Printed and bound in Canada

Dedication

To Judy—whose light still warms us.

CONTENTS

"And a tear, a real tear, trickled down his shabby
velvet nose and fell to the ground.
And then a strange thing happened. For where the
tear had fallen a flower grew out of the ground . . ."
MARGERY WILLIAMS, *The Velveteen Rabbit*

WHEN MY DEAR FRIEND WAS DYING OF BREAST CANCER AT
age thirty-seven, I felt helpless; nothing I could do would
prolong her life or give her even one more week with her
precious family.

When my neighbor's two young children were diagnosed
with diabetes, I felt helpless; she alone would face the sleep-
less nights of regulating blood-sugars and worrying about
needles and diabetic comas.

When my brother suddenly lost his dream job, I felt helpless; as much as I wanted to, I couldn't "fix it" for him or convince his employer he had made a big mistake in letting my brother go.

And when a good friend learned her son had been sexually abused by a former babysitter, I felt helpless; what could I possibly do to ease the bone-deep pain only a mother can feel for an innocent child so violated?

We've all experienced similar situations—when our hearts feel like breaking for a grief-stricken friend or relative, but our actions seem suddenly clumsy, our words empty. Usually our intentions are good at times like these—we rack our brains for the right thing to do or say. Give her a call? Write him a note? Stop by to talk? Send flowers? By the time we've exhausted the list of appropriate things to say or do, we often end up doing nothing. Inevitably, we see the person in the grocery store a few weeks later and instead of approaching her to express our condolences, we linger in the bread aisle and slip out hoping she doesn't see us. I've written this book so we'll never find ourselves in that position again.

In almost every situation where someone is in pain, there is something you can do! And most of the time, that something is fairly simple. As it turned out for me in each of the instances above, the most helpful thing I could do was to *listen*. Listening requires only a small investment of our time and attention, but pays tremendous dividends to those in need.

If it comes as a surprise that something as simple as listening is the universal healer, think about your own experiences with suffering. I can recall many times of personal sorrow— the death of my father, my husband's diagnosis of cancer, even concern over small things like finances, career, the unfairness of a son's teacher or a daughter's playmate—when being able to rely on a trusted friend as a sounding-board brought me more peace than being able to "fix" the problem, even if I could have.

Carolyn J. Rasmus, Ph.D., teaches about the healing power of listening. For her, it all began with the simple act of making bread:

One of the things I love to do when I have time off from work is to bake bread. I got carried away one afternoon and baked eight loaves instead of four. (There is something therapeutic about having my hands in dough. I think it replaces the mud we played in as children.) My friend, Kathryn, and I had planned to go to a movie that afternoon, and we had about thirty minutes before we were to leave the house. I said to Kathy, "It's going to take us a long time to eat eight loaves of bread. Why don't we take one over to the Campbells?" This was during a heated debate in the state legislature about teachers' salaries, and my across-the-street neighbor, Jim Campbell, was the focus of much of the controversy. We decided the Campbells could use a loaf of bread.

We rang the doorbell and Jim's wife came to the door.

As we handed her the bread, she started to cry. She said to us, "Please come in." I wondered what we would talk about, but I needn't have—all we had to do was listen.

When we left, we felt so good we said, "Let's give away another loaf of bread. We have time now before the second showing of the movie." Kathy and I debated about going to another neighbor's house because only two days before, their son had been convicted of a crime and was now in the state prison. What would we say to his parents? We didn't know, and I suppose, to be honest, we took the bread as an excuse because we didn't know how to start a conversation. We rang the doorbell. The father came to the door and said, "Please, please come in. Nobody has talked to us. We've got to talk to somebody." We listened for more than an hour to a mother and father, whose hearts were breaking, tell us about their son. When we got ready to leave, they hugged us. As we returned home Kathy said, "We missed the second showing, but who cares!"

A loaf of bread; a warm hug; a sensitive ear. Those are some of the most effective gifts you can give to those in need. And yes, there are other things you can do and say, as you'll learn in the following pages. You will discover just the right words to use in every situation—words that offer comfort, stories that uplift, poetry that encourages and inspires. You'll be reminded of simple ways to show love and compassion to others. And you'll read words of hope and healing that will buoy you up in your own moments of grief and sorrow.

Raymond Moody, in researching his book *Life After Life*, interviewed one hundred people who had died and returned to life. The accounts of each of their near-death experiences were stunning in their similarity: They had each followed a bright light and at the end were asked, "How have you loved and how have you served?"

As fascinating as this report is, I doubt that most of us are motivated to "love and serve" in order to amass a full page of gold stars on some heavenly report card. I believe, rather, that most people feel their interconnectedness naturally, and come to realize that it is only by loving each other—by reaching out with gentleness and kindness—that they ever really live.

Albert Schweitzer said, "Sometimes our light goes out but is blown into flame by another human being. Each of us owes our deepest thanks to those who have rekindled this light." Whether it is your own light that has gone out for a time, or that of a friend's, the words in this book can provide a spark to re-ignite the flame.

CHAPTER 1

Compassion and Friendship

"Grief knits two hearts in closer bonds than happiness ever can; and common sufferings are far stronger links than common joys."

ALPHONSE DE LAMARTINE

A LITTLE GIRL VISITED A NEIGHBOR'S HOUSE where her young friend had died.

"Why did you go there?" questioned her father.
"To comfort her mother," she said.
"What could you do to comfort her?"
"I climbed into her lap and cried with her," she said.

When a friend or loved one is in pain, you experience the pain too. That's one of the blessings of close relationships. It's also one of the responsibilities. To empathize with others, to develop sensitivity to their struggles, and to help the unfortunate are all hallmarks of true friendship. And by sharing our own problems with others, by being vulnerable, we give them the opportunity to really know and love us.

At different times in our lives, we'll find ourselves on both sides of this equation—the giving end and the receiving end. It's important to understand how to do both—to give generously and receive graciously—but of the two, we will gain the most personal satisfaction and joy from giving. To understand the hidden anguish in the hearts of those around us and get close enough to see the source of their tears will not only be of comfort to the person in need, but will enlarge our spirits as well. Life becomes richer and more rewarding when we reach out and touch others—more so than from almost any other human endeavor.

There are residual benefits, too, from being compassionate. Author Jeri-Lynn Johnson tells about a time Dr. Karl Menninger, the famous psychiatrist, gave a lecture on mental health and was answering questions from the audience. "What would you advise a person to do," asked one man, "if that person felt a nervous breakdown coming on?" Most people expected him to reply, "Consult a psychiatrist." To their astonishment, the doctor replied, "Lock up your house, go across the railroad tracks, find someone in need, and do something for that person."

My wife died after many years of complications from diabetes. A few months after her death, our wedding anniversary rolled around and I dreaded facing the day. I received a card in the mail that afternoon from our married daughter—not an anniversary card, but just a note telling me she was so glad I had married such a wonderful woman and how much she missed her. It made my day easier.

~ CLYDE

The more blossoms we cut off the rose bush in our garden to give away, the more buds develop on the stem. Likewise, the more we give of ourselves to others, the fuller our own lives become. But giving of oneself is not always as easy as pruning roses. To make friends and loved ones a priority in our life takes time, thoughtful consideration, and energy, and to cultivate relationships with openness and sincerity is not always convenient in our busy lives. The rewards, however, of the moments spent easing a child's aching heart, wiping the brow of a terminally ill patient, or being there at three in the morning when someone's world falls apart are greater than any comfort or convenience life has to offer.

For some people, having compassion for others is the easy part; it is treating themselves with care and concern that seems more difficult. If we strive to live by the Golden Rule in our relationships with family and friends, we must also apply it in a personal way, treating ourselves as we would want others to treat us. By taking care of ourselves physically and mentally, acknowledging that our ideas and feelings are important, our choices will inevitably be more thoughtful, practical, and wise. By treating ourselves well, we will be able to give to others more freely, and for the right reasons.

On the street I saw a small girl, cold and shivering in a thin dress, with little hope of a decent meal. I became angry and said to God, "Why did you permit this? Why don't you do something about it?" For a while God said nothing . . . then he said, "I certainly did do something about it, I made you."

~ Author Unknown

When each of my babies was christened, I always made a special cake with their name and the date on it to celebrate the occasion. With my third child, we were simply out of money and I felt sad there would be no "Christening cake" on their special day, although I mentioned it to no one. As our family sat down to eat dinner that evening, the doorbell rang, and there stood a friend with a beautiful cake in her hands. She ran a small cake-decorating business and had decided to deliver one to our family that day. I felt like she was an answer to my secret prayer.

⁓ HANNAH

"Tis easy enough to be pleasant,
When life flows along like a song"
But the man worthwhile is the one who will smile
When everything goes dead wrong.

⁓ Ella Wheeler Wilcox

Endow the living with the Tears
You squander on the Dead.

~◌ Emily Dickinson

Search for God

I sought His love in lore of books,
    In charts of science's skill;
They left me orphaned as before—
    His love eluded still;
Then in despair I breathed a prayer;
The Lord of Love was standing there!

I sought His love in sun and stars,
    And where the wild seas roll,
And found it not. As mute I stood,
    Fear overwhelmed my soul;
But when I gave to one in need,
I found the Lord of Love indeed.

~◌ Thomas Curtis Clark

If a friend of mine . . . gave a feast, and did not invite me to it, I should not mind a bit . . . But if . . . a friend of mine had a sorrow and refused to allow me to share it, I should feel it most bitterly. If he shut the doors of the house of mourning against me, I would move back again and again and beg to be admitted, so that I might share in what I was entitled to share. If he thought me unworthy, unfit to weep with him, I should feel it as the most poignant humiliation, as the most terrible mode by which disgrace could be inflicted on me . . . he who can look on the loveliness of the world and share its sorrow, and realize something of the owner of both, is in immediate contact with divine things, and has got as near to God's secret as any one can get.

∽ Oscar Wilde

He who waits to do a great deal of good at once will never do anything.

∽ Samuel Johnson

If I can stop one heart from breaking,
I shall not live in vain;
If I can ease one life the aching,
Or cool one pain,
Or help one fainting robin
Unto his nest again,
I shall not live in vain.

~ Emily Dickinson

---

*My husband had a massive heart attack but was recovering nicely
when, several months later, we attended a family reunion. As we
came out of our camper one morning, there were hundreds of red
paper hearts on wooden sticks planted in the ground all around us.
Each heart had a written message of love from a grandchild,
cousin, aunt, or uncle, and there was a big sign hanging on the front
door that said, "You've been heart-attacked!" We laughed and cried
and felt so loved, we left the hearts up the whole weekend.*

~ RUTH

Fresh Crab and French Bread

It was a typical winter day in San Francisco, cool and damp. We had lived there a few years before and were back renewing memories. Seeing the large, steaming crab vats as we walked along Fisherman's Wharf, I exclaimed, "Oh, let's take some crab home to Emma."

"Crab?" asked my husband. "Why crab?"

"I don't know. Maybe she would enjoy it."

Sensing my ever-present desire to bring cheer to a grieving widow in our neighborhood, Ron counseled me to find a more easily transported gift. He suggested that we find something more suitable in one of the souvenir shops beckoning us.

In and out of the shops we went, searching in vain for just the right memento. Empty-handed and tired, we started for our car, only to pass the crab vats once more.

"Ron, I still want to take some crab to Emma," I pleaded.

He was still resistant to hauling crab 150 miles, especially when I wasn't even sure Emma liked it. Nevertheless, we asked the vendor about transporting unrefrigerated crab that distance.

Soon we were crossing the Bay Bridge with the crab carefully wrapped in many thicknesses of paper; a long loaf of the Wharf's famous French bread was tucked in the side of the sack.

On the trip home my thoughts turned to Emma. I thought about her husband Ed, and remembered how shocked we were to hear about his fatal heart attack ten months before. Ed was a gifted surgeon, highly respected in our community. His passing was felt deeply. In addition to Emma, he left six children, the youngest just a toddler.

Though many grieved with the family, it was difficult for them to express their sympathy because Emma was extremely reserved and quiet. Few knew her well. As the months went on, her sorrow did not seem to lessen. Grief and poor health led to her withdrawing from activity outside her home.

I was determined to be her friend, and not let fear or personal rejection dilute my concern. Each week I went to her home, sometimes to be invited in while she shared her heartache. Other times she met me at the door but quickly terminated the visit with, "Thank you for coming."

As I rang the doorbell that day I could hear many feet running to answer. The door opened. Emma, surrounded by her children, stood there puzzled at my brown sack and protruding loaf of bread.

"Yes?" she inquired.

My spirits were dampened by her coolness, but I faked enthusiasm over our trip to the city and the gift we had brought.

As she took the fresh crab and French bread, Emma asked, "Is this for any special occasion?"

"No," I replied, "I just thought you might enjoy some crab from the Wharf."

"Thank you very much," she said, expressionless, and closed the door.

I returned to the car and slumped down into the seat, deflated. All I could say to Ron was, "I'm not sure Emma likes crab." We finished the drive home in silence.

Two days later came the following letter:

My dear friends:

I was very touched by your kind gesture last night and feel compelled to share a few thoughts with you.

Yesterday morning began with the usual daily tasks. I was out sweeping the walks when I looked up to the heavens and, noting the vast, billowing, white clouds, asked, "Ed, do you know what day this is? Do dates have a meaning in heaven? Can you possibly know how much I love you and how desperately you are missed; how I long to be taken into your strong arms and held again just for a minute?"

With tear-stained cheeks I wanted to know if he remembered twenty-three years ago, or even two years ago this day.

All day long memories came rushing back. I remembered our first trip to San Francisco and how cold it was as we walked by the steaming crab pots at the Wharf. Ed was so handsome in his Navy uniform. He always took my hand in his, and holding it tight placed both in his overcoat pocket. How comforting the warmth was. I could see him sitting in the cable car, with his boyish grin, a loaf of bread and a crab under each arm. So many times he repeated this procedure.

San Francisco was our playground. I cannot begin to count the number of seminars and scientific meetings we attended there. To learn more was almost a disease with Ed. After each session we always ended our stay by going to the Wharf. A loaf of bread and a fresh crab became symbolic of a wonderful time together. Now that he's gone, I wonder what mysteries of heaven he is exploring, what avenues are being opened to him. So many unanswered questions . . . so impatient I am.

Yesterday was a difficult day to get through. In late afternoon a beautiful floral arrangement arrived with a card from the children declaring their love for me. It was heartwarming. As I looked at the two little ones, then at Eddie and Janet, Miriam and David, I could see a part of Ed in each and realized that my cup runneth over.

Then at the close of day when I opened the door and saw you standing there with a loaf of bread and a package of fresh crab, it was like a direct message. You denied knowing it was a special day. Therefore I felt it was Ed's way of saying, "Happy anniversary. I do remember."

As ever,
Emma

~ Garnee Faulkner

My good friend was in the hospital after a hysterectomy. I wanted to visit and bring her flowers, but I was too broke at the time— even for flowers. So I picked up two 5 lb. bags of Pillsbury flour at the grocery store and tied them together with a big ribbon. When I walked in to her hospital room with "flours" that day, she not only smiled (laughing still hurt!) but I think she remembered it for years.

~ KRISTEN

If I Had Known

If I had known what trouble you were bearing;
What griefs were in the silence of your face;
I would have been more gentle, and more caring,
And tried to give you gladness for a space.
I would have brought more warmth into the place,
  If I had known.
If I had known what thoughts despairing drew you;
(Why do we never try to understand?)
I would have lent a little friendship to you,
And slipped my hand within your hand,
And made your stay more pleasant in the land
  If I had known.

~ Mary Carolyn Davies

Here's to you, old friend, may you live a thousand years.
Just to sort of cheer things in this vale of human tears;
And may I live a thousand too—a thousand less a day,
'Cause I wouldn't care to be on earth and hear you'd
    passed away.

〜 Anonymous

When we do the best we can we never know what miracle
is wrought in our life, or in the life of another.

〜 Helen Keller

When you're in pain, I'm in pain. That's part of being
a friend.

〜 Shai

Love Is as Love Does

When we take an extra step
or walk an extra mile,
we do so in opposition to the inertia of laziness
or the resistance of fear.

Moving out against laziness we call work;
moving out in the face of fear we call courage.
Love, then, is a form of work or a form of courage.

Since it requires the extension of ourselves,
love is always either work or courage.
If an act is not one of work or courage,
then it is not an act of love.
There are no exceptions.

∽ M. Scott Peck
The Road Less Traveled

Whenever you see a job to do, ask yourself these two questions: If not by me—whom? If not now—when?

∽ Arthur Lagueux

Lord, make me an instrument of Your peace.
Where there is hatred let me sow love;
Where there is injury, pardon;
Where there is doubt, faith;
Where there is despair, hope;
Where there is darkness, light, and
Where there is sadness, joy.

O divine Master,
Grant that I may not so much
Seek to be consoled as to console;
To be understood as to understand;
To be loved as to love;
For it is in giving that we receive;
It is in pardoning that we are pardoned, and
In dying that we are born to eternal life.

~ St. Francis of Assisi

The Account

Imagine there is a bank that credits your account each morning with $1,440. It carries over no balance from day to day. Every evening it deletes whatever part of the balance you failed to use during the day. What would you do? Draw out every cent, of course.

Each of us has such a bank. Its name is time. Every morning, it credits you with 1,440 minutes. Every night it writes off, as lost, whatever of this you have failed to invest to good purpose.

It carries over no balance. It allows no overdraft. Each day it opens a new account for you. Each night it burns the remains of the day. If you fail to use the day's deposits, the loss is yours. There is no going back. There is no drawing against the "tomorrow."

You must live in the present on today's deposits. Invest it to get the utmost in health, happiness and success from it.

The clock is ticking. Make the most of today.

∽ Author Unknown

Prerequisite

I prayed for strength when life pulsed low
Until God answered me:
"Go, lift the load of weary ones
Then I will strengthen thee."

I asked for courage when hope despaired,
Then came a voice benign:
"Inspire with faith thy brother's soul,
And I'll inspire thine."

I longed for light when darkness made
Me stumble through the night:
"Thy lamp held high for others' feet
Will make thy pathway bright."

I prayed that wisdom, talent, skill
Increased their meager store:
"First, share the portions that you have,
And I will give thee more."

At length I learned that blessings sought,
And help for which I pray,
Are only mine when shed abroad
And given, first away.

∽ Leila Grace Bassford

The Traveling Smile

I sat on a San Francisco bus going home, tired and depressed after one of those days when nothing seemed to go quite right. It was rush hour, and the bus was packed with people—dull-eyed, tired, aching, and short-tempered.

A large, package-laden lady got on the bus. Every seat was taken, so she had to stand in the aisle near me. War horse, I thought as I looked at her drawn and bitter face. That was a pretty good description.

Seated across the aisle next to her was a small, plain-looking lady, someone you wouldn't ordinarily notice. She looked up at "War Horse" and her face was lit with a smile. "Could I hold your packages?" she asked. "It's so hard to stand when your arms are full."

The woman glowered in confusion and looked away. But when she looked back, the smile was still there. Her wrinkled brow eased some as she handed over the packages. "They are very heavy," she said. "There are two pairs of specially made shoes for my crippled son, and they weigh twenty pounds a pair." She paused, and the next words seemed very hard for her to say: "Thank you." They chatted on, and as they did, she smiled. Her whole face softened and her body relaxed.

Soon the seated lady got off and the other woman sat down in her place. But her expression had changed, and she smiled up at the young coed standing above her.

"Could I hold your books for you? It's difficult to hold on with books sliding every which way."

The girl smiled back, and as she gave up her books I heard her ask, "Did I hear you say you have a son who goes to Jefferson? That's where I go to school."

I had to get off at the next stop, but I imagined that smile traveling all over San Francisco. I too smiled, and wasn't so tired anymore.

~ Jane Bunker Newcomb

We live in deeds, not years; in thoughts, not breaths;
In feelings, not in figures on a dial.
We should count time by heart-throbs.

~ Philip James Bailey

Whenever you're blue
Find something to do
For somebody else
Who's sadder than you.

～ Author Unknown

Trouble is a part of your life, and if you don't share it,
you don't give the person who loves you a chance to love
you enough.

～ Dinah Shore

When we admit our vulnerability, we include others; if we
deny it, we shut them out.

～ May Sarton

Listen

When I ask you to listen to me,
and you start giving advice,
you have not done what I asked.

When I ask you to listen to me,
and you begin to tell me why I shouldn't
feel that way, you are trampling on my feelings.

When I ask you to listen to me,
and you feel you have to do something
to solve my problem, you have failed me—
strange as that may seem.

Listen! All I ask is that you listen
not talk, or do—just hear me.

Advice is cheap. Twenty-five cents will
get you both Dear Abby and Billy Graham
in the same newspaper.

And I can do for myself; I'm not helpless . . .
maybe discouraged and faltering,
but not helpless.

When you do something for me
that I can and need to do for myself,
you contribute to my fear and weakness.

But, when you accept as a simple fact
that I do feel what I feel (no matter how irrational),
then I can quit trying to convince you
and get about the business of understanding
what's behind this irrational feeling.

And when that's clear, the answers
are obvious, and I don't need advice.
Irrational feelings make sense when
we understand what's behind them.

So, please listen and just hear me.
And, if you want to talk, wait a minute for your turn;
and I'll listen to you.

~ Author Unknown

Seeds of Love

Last fall I was away from my home during the period of time when it would have been nice to plant tulip bulbs and daffodils. I felt a bit sad as I looked at the dark earth and realized that no bulbs would burst forth and announce spring. But on my birthday, in the middle of March, I walked out into my front yard and saw three daffodils. I wondered how that happened. I didn't remember planting daffodils. When did they come up?

The next day I found more daffodils and before long discovered tulips! They sprang up every day in different places, and every morning I ran out to see what was coming up out of my ground, which to my knowledge was void of bulbs or seeds.

Those seeds of love had been planted in the fall by a friend. Different plants continued coming up to delight and surprise me for about two weeks, and then a little card arrived that said, "Happy Birthday! I thought the flowers would be an announcement for spring and wanted to share spring with you this year."

What a surprise. What a gift of love and service.

~ Ardeth G. Kapp

38

My mother was 85 years old and my father was in a nursing home. I tried to call Mother often and sent her things from time to time. I mailed her a little calendar that had some pages labeled, "Thank You Notes to God," with blank lines numbered one through thirty. I didn't think she'd pay any attention to those pages, but at one point, she ripped them out and mailed them to me. Here is the list she wrote—the small things that made a difference in her life:

A telephone call from Mildred
A visit from Anita
A magazine from Kay
A visit with a friendly person in the mall
My family
Carolyn's concern
Lunch at Kay's
A call from Mark
A call from Evelyn
A call from Vera
A visit from our cousins in Detroit
A day of rest
A telephone call from Anita
A card from Carolyn
Meals on wheels
A telephone call from Kay
I called a friend of a friend
I'm able to get around

I had a telephone visit with Mark
I'm thankful my sister can drive
Carolyn's call was what I needed

Each of the things my mother was thankful for cost little if any money and took practically no time. Each was a simple act of selfless service—people to people, face to face, eye to eye, voice to ear, heart to heart acts of love.

~ Carolyn J. Rasmus
    Women and the Power Within

The purpose of life is to increase the warm heart.
Think of other people. Serve other people sincerely.
No cheating …

~ Dalai Lama

My baby son was born with congenital heart problems and I spent weeks in the hospital with him, while my other children took over the other household duties. I was so tired and stressed most of the time, I could hardly keep track of time. When I opened the front door one Friday morning, there was a big pink box of donuts on the front step, with an anonymous "Happy Last Day of School!" written on top. It brightened my family's whole day.

~ MARYANNE

God does notice us, and he watches over us. But it is usually through another person that he meets our needs.

~ Spencer W. Kimball

Love is a verb.

~ Anonymous

Love is Being There

Many years ago, I noticed an interesting phenomenon in a hospital. Many of the dying patients began to feel wonderful; not so much physically, but mentally. This wasn't because of me, but because of the cleaning woman. Every time she walked into the room of one of my dying patients, something would happen. I would have given a million dollars to learn that woman's secret.

Determined to know how she was making people feel good, I followed her around. After a few weeks of snooping around like this, she grabbed me and dragged me into a room behind the nurse's station. She told me how, some time ago, one of her six children had become very ill one winter. In the middle of the night she took her three-year-old son to the emergency room, where she sat with him on her lap, desperately waiting hours for the physician to come. But no one came, and she watched her little boy die of pneumonia, in her arms. She shared all this pain and agony without hate, without resentment, without anger, without negativity.

"Why are you telling me this?" I asked. "What has this to do with my dying patients?"

"Death is not a stranger to me anymore," she replied. "He is like an old acquaintance. Sometimes when I walk into the room of your dying patients, they look so scared. I can't help but walk over to them and touch them. I tell them I've seen death, and when it happens, they will be okay. And I just stay there with them. I may want to run, but I don't. I try to be there for the other person. That is love."

Unschooled in the ways of psychology and medicine, this woman knew one of the greatest secrets in life: love is being there, and caring.

~ Elizabeth Kubler-Ross
  Life Lessons

CHAPTER 2

Important Dos and Don'ts

"You must give some time to your fellow man.
Even if it's a little thing, do something for those
who have need of help, something for which you
get no pay but the privilege of doing it."

ALBERT SCHWEITZER

DURING DIFFICULT TIMES, A GOOD FRIEND IS
the best medicine there is. What we as friends
do and say during those times greatly affects
our loved one's ability to heal. Even if we feel awkward or
stumble over words, our good intentions will usually be
appreciated and will be a visible sign of our concern. And
occasionally, even a small gesture—a smile, a hug, or an
encouraging word—will be just the thing to turn the tide.

Here are some things to think about as you go about comforting, serving, sympathizing, and loving:

♻ *Important Actions*

❦ Think of the three B's: Be sensitive, Be available, Be QUIET. Listen more than you talk. Those experiencing grief or loss heal best by talking about it—sometimes over and over again. Listen patiently without judging or giving advice.

❦ Offer a hug or simple touch; hands often speak as voices cannot. When a touch is warmly offered—whether it's holding a hand, rubbing a shoulder, or simply saying "I've come to help you cry"—it imparts a tangible source of strength.

❦ The word "comfort" comes from two Latin words: "com" and "fortis" meaning, "strengthened by being with." Be there. Run errands, help with household chores, provide child care. Many times, people in crisis are in a state of shock and have difficulty keeping up with the normal routines of life. They may not ask for help, but do specific tasks for them anyway.

❦ Send a card—cards are like hugs through the mail. Make it personal, and in the case of a death, add a short note about a special memory you have of the departed. Use an appropriate quote or poem from this book to make it even more personal.

* Creating a sense of outer well-being helps the body and soul work together in healing. Buy a set of new pillows or sheets for the person in pain. Get them a massage or facial—whatever feels good physically.

* Give a gift of a journal. Studies show that people who write about their feelings are less depressed and healthier than those who don't.

* If your friend or someone in his or her family is in the hospital, ask how you can help with the normal routine at home. Offer to take the kids to the park, go grocery shopping, arrange for meals to be brought in, take care of pets or houseplants, pick up mail, mow the lawn, and so on.

* When there has been a death, try to remember the "forgotten mourners" with a card or flowers. Often when a child dies, people forget that siblings and grandparents will grieve. Think of others who might be affected by the loss. Give a gift of a small tree to plant in the loved one's memory.

* Laughter, even in the midst of tragedy, prevents people from becoming stuck in depression. Give a gift of a favorite comedy video or DVD, and suggest you watch it together.

❧ Offer to go walking with your friend. Spending even fifteen minutes a day in the sunshine can lift one's spirits and guard one against depression.

❧ Pets fill a special role for many people—they offer unconditional love—and the loss of a pet can be a very emotional experience. Be sensitive to those dealing with this kind of sadness; sending a card or little token of remembrance is not inappropriate.

❧ Thomas Moore writes, "The soul is nurtured by beauty. What food is to the body, pleasing images are to the soul." Give a basket with fresh flowers, offer to take your friend to an art museum or to browse through a bookstore, or have a picnic by a lake. Give a gift of a lovely picture frame or a brightly colored tablecloth.

❧ After a loss of any kind, gently encourage your friend to return to outside activities after a few weeks or months. Suggest lunch or a movie as relief from the isolation of grief. If he or she turns you down, accept it but don't give up trying.

❧ When a friend is sick, deliver a get-well "indulgence basket" filled with bedside comforts: something irresistible to read, cough drops, tissues, assorted fruit teas, homemade soup, a loaf of banana-nut bread, a small, flowering plant.

❧ When there has been a death in the family, especially in the case where someone is left widowed (or recently divorced), weekends and holidays are particularly lonely and difficult. Reaching out to people on these occasions is very comforting: Invite them to join a family outing; offer to help get out Christmas ornaments and decorate their tree; invite them to your Thanksgiving dinner. Or simply send a card to let them know you're especially thinking about them at that time of year.

❧ Don't forget the caretaker. If your friend has assumed the role of caretaker for an elderly or chronically ill relative, his or her life is likely to be emotionally exhausting. Send a card, drop by and offer to do an errand, pick up medicine or supplies, bring a pot of soup or loaf of bread, or purchase a massage for your friend. A caretaker has very little time to think of him- or herself and will appreciate your concern.

❧ Pray for your friends or loved ones who are sad, distressed, or grieving. It will benefit both them and you.

2. *When the Person in Need Is You*

❧ Think about living for the present. Concentrate on what you have to achieve today instead of wallowing in past regrets or worrying about the future. As you start setting daily goals, you'll eventually be able to develop long-term plans.

❧ Realize that all your feelings are valid and need to be experienced, accepted, and expressed. Find a trusted friend who will listen to your anger, guilt, and discouragement without judging you.

❧ Keep decisions—especially major ones—to a bare minimum during a tragedy or loss. Allow yourself several months or a year of recovery, at which time you'll be more able to think clearly and assess your situation.

❧ Be good to yourself. Play hooky. Take a day off from work and splurge at a spa. Get your hair highlighted, have a pedicure, a massage. Indulge in physical luxuries you wouldn't normally allow yourself.

❧ Touching the earth can help put things in perspective and reminds us that we are all connected to each other: climb a rock, pick flowers, work in the garden, build a snowman, run through the sand at the beach. For that matter, build a sand castle.

❧ If possible, exercise. Physical activity relieves stress. Even a ten-minute walk can be beneficial. Don't hesitate to call a friend to ask if he or she will join you.

❧ If you are dealing with a death, talk or pray to your deceased loved one. Visit the cemetery and talk out loud, or write a letter to them expressing your pain and loneliness, your anger and guilt.

❧ Instead of the typical advice, "Count your blessings," Thich Nhat Hanh suggests asking ourselves the question, "What's *not* wrong [with my life]?" Being aware of life's wholesome and healing wonders—the clear blue sky, a baby's laugh, the ability to sing or dance—can help bring us out of the prison of our sorrow.

❧ If possible, plan ahead for times of the year that will be most difficult. After you've experienced a loss, rather than letting a birthday, anniversary, or holiday sneak up on you, decide whether to celebrate it and in what manner. Think about options like going out to dinner, taking a trip, visiting friends, even working in a homeless shelter.

❧ Even in the midst of grief or despair, allow yourself to enjoy the people in your life and don't feel guilty about going out and having a good time, if you can. You deserve it.

𝒬   Important Words

Saying something is better than saying nothing, ignoring or avoiding the person who is suffering. "I'm so sorry" is a simple but very comforting thing to say to almost anyone.

If a spouse or child has died, share a memory of that person: "I remember when she . . . " or "He had a great talent for . . . " Talk about the deceased openly, remembering the joy and the life, and mentioning the person by name.

Avoid cliches such as "everything will be okay" or "try to look for the good in this situation." More sincere and appreciated words are:

- This must be very hard for you.

- It's okay to cry—cry as much as you need to.

- I can't imagine how hard this must be for you.

- I'll call tomorrow to see what I can do for you.

- I just heard about . . . and I don't even know what to say.

- You must be exhausted. Why don't you let me take care of . . . so you can get some sleep?

- I've never gone through what you're going through. I'm trying to put myself in your shoes, and I'm not sure I could handle it.

- You don't deserve this. I want you to know I'm thinking of you during this hard time.

- I'm so sad about . . . I sure wish there was a way I could lessen your pain.

- You're facing a hard thing—I really admire your courage.

- I trust you—I know you'll make the right decision.

Creative, sensitive listening, interspersed with questions that show you care, can be most helpful.

A few years after I was married I became pregnant; my husband and I were very excited about having a baby. However, two months later, I had a miscarriage and found myself wondering if I'd ever be able to have children. When I returned to work, people avoided me, not knowing what to say or not thinking it was a big deal. I remember one co-worker who came over to my desk, bent down, and placed a sweet kiss on my cheek. He walked away without saying a word, but his gesture assured me that someone cared about me.

꧁ KATHLEEN

Without being rude or invasive, ask questions like:

- ❧ How are you holding up?

- ❧ Do you want to tell me what happened?

- ❧ Are you able to sleep? Are you afraid to be alone?

- ❧ Do you need me to make any calls or answer your phone?

- ❧ Do you need a ride to the doctor's or could I pick up medicine for you?

- ❧ Would you like to come over for dinner or could I bring you dinner?

- ❧ Could I watch your children for you or pick them up?

🎵 Important Don'ts

DON'T SAY: *"Call me if you need anything."*
A person suffering a loss or tragedy probably won't call. It is best to take the initiative and do something for them without their asking for help.

DON'T SAY: *"I know how you feel."*
It is very difficult to comprehend the depth of the loss or the same feelings of despair unless you have experienced a very similar situation. A lack of sincerity will be felt.

DON'T SAY: *"Have you reached closure yet?"*
This suggests that your friend ought to be able to move on and put things to rest when he or she may not be at that stage yet.

DON'T SAY: *"You'll eventually heal/recover."*
This implies that a cure or a resolution is possible, when, in fact, it might not seem imaginable at the time, and the comment will only increase guilt feelings that may already be present.

DON'T SAY: *"It was God's will. You'll be a stronger person for this tragedy."*
While there may be some truth to this, this response tends to minimize the person's loss or grief. The person can't imagine why God would want to cause such pain and it's no comfort to be told that the tragedy will make him or her a better person someday. There will be plenty of time for

philosophizing in the years to come, but it's the last thing a person wants to hear when in the middle of a crisis.

DON'T SAY: *"You should"* or *"you shouldn't"* (*be angry, be jealous, be resentful, cry so much, take the child's pictures down, throw your ex-husband's clothes or books away, and so on*).
People think and do irrational things in difficult times, and it is best not to make judgments or make them feel guilty. Everyone has different ways of dealing with their problems and what they really need is your understanding and support.

DON'T SAY: *"Your situation reminds me of when . . . "*
It's not comforting to tell self-serving stories of family or friends, and your experience almost never sounds similar to what a person in pain is going through.

DON'T SAY: *"You need to get on with your life . . . you can remarry . . . you can try to get pregnant again in a few months . . . there are plenty of other jobs out there . . . "* and so on.
Each person is different and getting over their grief will take as long as it takes. Instead, you might encourage your friends to get counseling or join a support group if they seem to be "stuck" in their depression or pain too long.

DON'T SAY: *"Time will heal."*
It may not.

CHAPTER 3

The Lessons of Adversity

"You can't be brave if you've only had wonderful
things happen to you."

MARY TYLER MOORE

One thing is certain about life: it will always be
full of problems. None of us can escape discouragement or disappointment at times, frustration
and heartache at others. Some people have to cope with
chronic disease or crippling accidents. Others are single or
widowed and live empty lives of loneliness. Many experience
the devastation of divorce, the struggle of dealing with
difficult or wayward children, the stress of heavy workloads,
the depression of job loss. As soon as we've surmounted one
crisis, another presents itself until we sometimes feel that the

sun is falling out of the sky, pulling down a curtain of darkness with it. As Carole Baker said, "Life seems to be a never-ending series of survivals."

Even small, everyday irritations—delays, moments of anger, feelings of rejection, financial worries, traffic jams, and deadlines—sap us of our energy and joy. And so, the questions keep going through our minds, even though we've reckoned with them a million times before: Why me? What did I do to deserve this? Am I being punished for some reason? Why can't my life be as easy as my neighbor's? When do I get a break? When does the fun part begin?

Sometimes the only thing to fall back on in the midst of tribulation is the ancient truth, "This too shall pass." Experience tells us it works with our children: we observe each stage of their development and wonder, "Will he ever get past the 'terrible twos'?" or "When will she move past this self-obsessed teenage phase?" And we're relieved when they do, in fact, move on. Likewise, we must recognize that almost every obstacle in our path will one day fade and seem less tragic. Knowing this helps us to view adversity as an ally instead of an enemy, and even helps us understand how we can grow stronger from it.

The great violin maker, Stradivari, was once asked how long it takes to make a good violin. He answered, "A thousand years. Violins made from young trees which are shielded from the storm can never be fashioned into masterpieces. A thousand years are necessary to strengthen and try the trees

When my wife, Laura, found out she only had a few months to live, our children were 6 and 9 years old. She was very weak, but wanted to leave some things behind for the children, to remind them of her after she was gone. Her friend sent a package to Laura of specially chosen birthday cards—enough to be given to both children on each of their birthdays up through age 16. With much difficulty but much love, Laura wrote a message on each card and gave them to me, to distribute each year.

~ PETE

---

that can be made into fine instruments—they must stand the wind and tempest, sleet and snow, heat and fire."

When your loved ones find themselves in the eye of the storm, it's very difficult to see how the experience can eventually make them better and stronger—that fact is usually the last thing they want to hear or think about. For the moment, it's best to listen, to talk things through, to encourage baby steps, and to offer loving support and an understanding heart. If the person in need is you, remember that you are not alone. There are those around you willing and waiting to help ease your burden if you will just let them in.

The Weaving

My life is but a weaving
Between my Lord and me;
I cannot choose the colors
He worketh steadily.
Ofttimes He weaveth sorrow
And I in foolish pride
Forget that He seeth the upper,
And I the underside.
Not till the loom is silent
And the shuttles cease to fly,
Shall God unroll the canvas
And explain the reason why.
The dark threads are as needful
In the Weaver's skillful hand,
As the threads of gold and silver
In the pattern He has planned.

～ Author Unknown

Every adversity is an adventure.
Every pain is a pilgrimage.
Every trial is a trail.
Every problem is a path.
Every load is a road.
Every hurt is on the move.
It's leading you somewhere.
Where is it taking you?

~ Robert H. Schuller
  Turning Hurts into Halos

In December of 1914 the great Edison Industries factory in
West Orange, New Jersey, was nearly completely destroyed
by fire. In one night Thomas Edison lost some $2 million
worth of scientific equipment and records of much of his
life's work. The following morning, as he walked about the
charred embers that remained, the 67-year-old Edison was
quoted as saying, "There is great value in disaster. All our
mistakes are burned up. Thank God we can start anew."

After my divorce, my teenage daughter had a rough time adjusting. She spent a lot of time in her room listening to music and talking to friends on the phone or e-mail. I tried to keep the lines of communication open between us but I was grateful she had good friends to confide in also. I remember one night, her best friend came over with a home-made chocolate cake. Sticking out of the top was a note saying, "I've GAINED so much from our friendship—now it's YOUR turn!" It felt good to laugh.

~ STACEY

The Sunflower

Of course you have clouds.
What mortal sky does not?
Only in heaven
Are the heavens clear forever.

It's all right.
I am a sunflower.
I will find the light.

~ Carol Lynn Pearson

Beauty from Sorrow

Elizabeth Barrett Browning's parents disapproved so strongly of her marriage to Robert Browning that they disowned her. Almost weekly Elizabeth wrote letters of love to her mother and father, asking for a reconciliation. They never once replied. After ten years of letter writing, Elizabeth received a huge box in the mail. She opened it and to her dismay and heartbreak, the box contained all of her letters to her parents. Not one of them had ever been opened. Today those love letters are among the most beautiful in classical English literature. Had her parents opened and read only a few of them, a reconciliation might have been effected, and the world would never have known the beauty of her words.

The Gardener and the Currant Bush

In the early dawn, a young gardener was pruning his trees and shrubs. He had one choice currant bush which had gone too much to wood. He feared therefore that it would produce little, if any, fruit.

Accordingly, he trimmed and pruned the bush and cut it back. In fact, when he had finished, there was little left but stumps and roots.

Tenderly he considered what was left. It looked so sad and deeply hurt. On every stump there seemed to be a tear where the pruning knife had cut away the growth of early spring. The poor bush seemed to speak to him, and he thought he heard it say:

"Oh, how could you be so cruel to me; you who claim to be my friend, who planted me and cared for me when I was young, and nurtured me and encouraged me to grow? Could you not see that I was rapidly responding to your care? I was nearly half as large as the trees across the fence, and might soon have become like one of them. But now you've cut my branches back; the green, attractive leaves are gone, and I am in disgrace among my fellows."

The young gardener looked at the weeping bush and heard its plea with sympathetic understanding. His voice was full of kindness as he said, "Do not cry; what I have done to you was necessary that you might be a prize currant bush in my garden. You were not intended to give shade or shelter by your branches. My purpose when I planted you was

64

that you should bear fruit. When I want currants, a tree, regardless of its size, cannot supply the need.

"No, my little currant bush, if I had allowed you to continue to grow as you had started, all your strength would have gone to wood; your roots would not have gained a firm hold, and the purpose for which I brought you into my garden would have been defeated. Your place would have been taken by another, for you would have been barren. You must not weep; all this will be for your good; and some day, when you see more clearly, when you are richly laden with luscious fruit, you will thank me and say, 'Surely, he was a wise and loving gardener. He knew the purpose of my being, and I thank him now for what I then thought was cruelty.'"

Some years later, this young gardener was in a foreign land, and he himself was growing. He was proud of his position and ambitious for the future.

One day an unexpected vacancy entitled him to promotion. The goal to which he had aspired was now almost within his grasp, and he was proud of the rapid growth which he was making.

But for some reason unknown to him, another was appointed in his stead, and he was asked to take another post relatively unimportant and which, under the circumstances, caused his friends to feel that he had failed.

The young man staggered to his tent and knelt beside his cot and wept. He now knew that he could never hope to have what he had thought so desirable. He cried to God and said, "Oh, how could you be so cruel to me? You who claim to be my friend—you who brought me here and nurtured and encouraged me to grow. Could you not see that I was almost equal to the other men whom I have so long admired? But now I have been cut down. I am a disgrace among my fellows. Oh, how could you do this to me?"

He was humiliated and chagrinned and a drop of bitterness was in his heart, when he seemed to hear an echo from the past. Where had he heard those words before? They seemed familiar. Memory whispered: "I'm the gardener here."

He caught his breath. Ah, that was it—the currant bush! But why should that long-forgotten incident come to him in the midst of his hour of tragedy? And memory answered with words which he himself had spoken:

"Do not cry . . . what I have done to you was necessary . . . you were not intended for what you sought to be, . . . if I had allowed you to continue . . . you would have failed in the purpose for which I planted you and my plans for you would have been defeated. You must not weep; some day when you are richly laden with experience you will say, 'He was a wise gardener. He knew the purpose of my earth life, . . . I thank him now for what I thought was cruel.'"

His own words were the medium by which his prayer was answered. There was not bitterness in his heart as he humbly spoke again to God and said, "I know you now. You are the gardener, and I the currant bush. Help me dear God to endure the pruning, and to grow as you would have me grow; to take my allotted place in life and evermore say, 'Thy will not mine be done.'"

~ Hugh B. Brown
  Eternal Quest

On my first wedding anniversary, I found out I had breast cancer. After my mastectomy, my husband brought me home from the hospital and I was naturally apprehensive about him seeing my body. Tired and emotionally exhausted, I lay down on the bed to rest and my husband laid down next to me. Without a word, he gently kissed my new scar to reassure me that his love was more than skin-deep. It was a moment I'll never forget.

~ LAUREL

Thou art never at any time nearer to God than when under tribulation, which he permits for the purification and beautifying of the soul.

~ Molinos

Expect trouble as an inevitable part of life and repeat to yourself the most comforting words of all: This, too, shall pass.

~ Ann Landers

After my wife was killed in an automobile accident, I especially mourned for my three teenage daughters who would grow up without a mother. A friend at church arranged for 30 or 40 of my wife's friends to write letters about her as an adult and then presented a scrapbook full of the letters to my daughters, so they would know something about their mother as a woman.

~ MICHAEL

God whispers to us in our pleasures, speaks in our conscience, but shouts in our pains: it is His megaphone to rouse a deaf world.

~ C. S. Lewis

Sorrows are our best educators. A person can see further through a tear than a telescope.

If you train yourself to rejoice in suffering, if you think that everything is done by God for one's own betterment and uplift, if you welcome pain as a messenger of God to make you remember Him . . . then pain will not be pain anymore. Suffering will not be suffering anymore.

~ Sivanda

Imagine yourself as a living house. God comes in to rebuild that house. At first, perhaps, you can understand what He is doing. He is getting the drains right and stopping the leaks in the roof and so on: you knew that those jobs needed doing and so you are not surprised. But presently he starts knocking the house about in a way that hurts abominably and does not seem to make sense. What on earth is He up to? The explanation is that He is building quite a different house from the one you thought of—throwing out a new wing here, putting on an extra floor there, running up towers, making courtyards. You thought you were going to be made into a decent little cottage but He is building a palace. He intends to come and live in it Himself.

~ C. S. Lewis
   Mere Christianity

Refining Fire

He sat by the fire of sevenfold heat
As he watched by the precious ore
And closer he bent with a turning gaze
As he heated it more and more.
He knew he had ore that could stand the test
And he wanted the finest gold
To mold as a crown for the king to wear
Set with gems with price untold.
So, he lit our gold in the burning fire
Though we fey would have said, "Nay,"
And he watched as the dross that we said
We had not seen was melted and passed it away.
And the gold grew brighter and yet more bright
But our eyes were filled with tears.

We saw but the fire, not the master's hand
And questioned with anxious fears.
Yet our gold shown out with a richer flow
As it mirrored a form above
That bent o'er the fire, though unseen by us
With the look of ineffable love.
Can we think that it pleases his loving heart
To cause us moments of pain?
No. But he saw through the present cross
The bliss of eternal gain.
So he waited there with a watchful eye
With a love that is strong and sure
And his goal did not suffer a bit more heat
Than was needed to make it pure.

~∽ Author Unknown

Pain stayed so long, I said to him today,
"I will not have you with me anymore,"
I stamped my foot and said, "Be on your way,"
And paused there, startled at the look he wore.
"I, who have been your friend," he said to me;
"I, who have been your teacher—all you know
Of understanding, love, of sympathy
And patience, I have taught you. Shall I go?"

~ Author Unknown

Yes, Charlotte. If we were given a preview of life's moments
of crisis, a chance to think instead of having to act in haste,
we would not have to go through life blaming ourselves for
not having acted properly. That is the big difference
between life and the theater. Rehearsals.

~ Aranka Siegal
Upon the Head of the Goat

The Monument

God,
Before He sent His children to earth
Gave each of them
A very carefully selected package
Of problems.

These,
He promised, smiling,
Are yours alone. No one
Else may have the blessings
These problems will bring you.

And only you
Have the special talents and abilities
That will be needed
To make these problems
Your servants.

Now go down to your birth
And to your forgetfulness. Know that
I love you beyond measure.
These problems that I give you
Are a Symbol of your
Love for me,
Your Father.

～ Blaine M. Yorgason
    Charlie's Monument

Our family had just moved several states away from our old home and we were feeling very alone in our new neighborhood. I'll never forget the night another family came to our door holding a plate of cookies. They had a couple of kids with them around our kids' ages and we invited them in. They ended up staying for a half-hour or so, telling us a little about their family, and just being friendly. It was a simple act of kindness, but it made a world of difference to us.

∽ STEPHEN

If you are discouraged it is a sign of pride because it shows you trust in your own power. Your self-sufficiency, your selfishness and your intellectual pride will inhibit His coming to live in your heart because God cannot fill what is already full. It is as simple as that.

∽ Mother Teresa
The Joy in Loving

Along the Road

I walked a mile with Pleasure;
She chattered all the way.
But left me none the wiser
For all she had to say.

I walked a mile with Sorrow.
And ne'er a word said she;
But oh, the things I learned from her
When Sorrow walked with me!

—Robert Browning

We fail to recognize that crisis and opportunity go hand in hand. In Chinese, the word crisis has two faces—two characters. The first character means "danger," but the second character means "opportunity."

God is the hardest taskmaster I have known on this earth, and he tries you through and through. And when you find that your faith is failing or your body is failing you, and you are sinking, he comes to your assistance somehow or other, and proves to you that you must not lose your faith—he is always at your beck and call, but on his terms, not on your terms. So I have found. I cannot really recall a single instance where he has forsaken me.

⌐ Mahatma Gandhi

Most putts don't drop. Most beef is tough. Most children grow up to be just people. Most successful marriages require a high degree of mutual toleration. Most jobs are more often dull than otherwise . . .

Life is like an old-time rail journey—delays, sidetracks, smoke, dust, cinders and jolts, interspersed only occasionally by beautiful vistas and thrilling bursts of speed. The trick is to thank the Lord for letting you have the ride.

⌐ Jenkins Lloyd Jones

Compensation

Enormous grief
Has leveled me—
Welded its bulk
To my back
And will not let
Me rise.

Yet—
"I'll give
No burden that
You cannot bear,"
He promised me.

I am amazed—
How strong my back
Must be.

∽ Carol Lynn Pearson

Don't surrender your loneliness
So quickly.
Let it cut more deep.

Let it ferment and season you
As few human
Or even divine ingredients can.

Something missing in my heart tonight
Has made my eyes so soft,
My voice
So tender,

My need of God
Absolutely
Clear.

∼ Hafiz

A Creed for Those Who Have Suffered

I asked God for strength, that I might achieve.
I was made weak, that I might learn humbly to obey . . .
I asked for health, that I might do great things.
I was given infirmity, that I might do better things . . .
I asked for riches, that I might be happy.
I was given poverty, that I might be wise . . .
I asked for power, that I might have the praise of men.
I was given weakness, that I might feel the need of God . . .
I asked for all things, that I might enjoy life.
I was given life, that I might enjoy all things . . .
I got nothing I asked for—but everything I had hoped for.
Almost despite myself, my unspoken prayers were answered.
I am, among men, most richly blessed!

∽ Roy Campanella

CHAPTER 4

Of Peace and Prayer

"Have you been asking God what He is going to do?
He will never tell you. God does not tell you what
He is going to do. He reveals to you who He is."

OSWALD CHAMBERS

We live in a noisy, confusing world where it takes a conscious effort to turn off all the commotion long enough to find the inner peace and serenity our souls need. At times of tragedy and sorrow, it's even more important to find our center, to create an openness to the moment that only comes through silence. This spiritual silence is what allows us to get out of God's way and surrender to Him, the kind of letting go that ultimately leads to healing, peace of mind, and serenity.

One way to arrive at this state is through prayer. Prayer is essential to our emotional well-being and spiritual growth because it helps us focus on something outside ourselves and forces us to put our thoughts, our concerns, our heartache into words. Whether we feel discouraged, angry, jealous, or despondent, prayer helps us get things off our chest and move on. By acknowledging a higher power, we're reminded that someone else is in charge, and we're comforted by knowing that we can turn a portion of our pain, at least, over to that power.

One of the beauties of prayer is that it is a portable resource—we can take advantage of it anytime, any place, in any circumstance. It's probably the only conversation in which you don't have to hold back; you can say whatever needs to be said, exactly the way you want to express it, without being judged. Prayer requires no set format or long memorized passages—talking to God should be as personal and natural as talking to a beloved parent or friend. The more comfortable we become with prayer, the more we appreciate the intimacy and communion associated with it. As a very wise eleven-year-old Cortni Smeltzer reminds us: "God has a lot of people talking to him at the same time. He listens to every one of them and doesn't even have call-waiting."

Aside from its psychological benefits, prayer can actually work. A team from New York's Columbia University was recently amazed to discover that prayer appeared to double the chances of conception in infertile couples. Among a group of women undergoing in vitro fertilization, those

My first child died of SIDS when she was one week old. We were away from home at my mother's house for Thanksgiving when she died. The funeral was scheduled for three days later and when I awoke that morning, a FedEx package arrived—a beautiful hand-made white dress, bonnet, and booties from my church friends at home. In my grief, I hadn't even thought about what to dress the baby in for her funeral, and I was so grateful to receive this gift of love from dear friends, who I later learned had worked around the clock to finish in time.

~ DENISE

who were prayed for (with neither the women nor their doctors knowing anyone was praying for them), enjoyed a 50 percent pregnancy rate, compared to a 26 percent pregnancy rate among those for whom no one prayed. The results were so astounding, in fact, that the doctors considered whether they were even publishable because no one could explain it. (It was finally published in the *Journal of Reproductive Medicine*.)

"Do you want an impenetrable sense of inner peace?" asks Christopher H. Jackson. "Take a deep breath . . . let go of anxiety . . . ask God to lift the clouds of doubt and fear from your vision. Believe that peace is your natural state."

Through quiet meditation and simple yet heartfelt prayer, we will find the hope that comes from knowing that ultimately, our lives are in more capable hands than our own. That understanding will come to each of us at different times, in very different and personal ways. As Ralph Waldo Emerson reminds us, "God enters by a private door into every individual."

In the case of a friend or loved one who is dealing with adversity, offer to pray with that person, pray for the person, teach the person how to pray, or add his or her name to a prayer circle. Talk to the person about the healing power of prayer and remind him or her of what Tennyson once wrote: "More things are wrought by prayer than this world dreams of."

In the clumsy move
From prayer
To telephone,
I suddenly know
(though with less comfort)
that God
is in the ringing.

～ Edwina Gately
    A Mystical Heart

You can talk to God because God listens. Your voice matters in heaven. He takes you very seriously. When you enter his presence, the attendants turn to you to hear your voice. No need to fear that you will be ignored. Even if you stammer or stumble, even if what you have to say impresses no one, it impresses God—and he listens . . .

Intently. Carefully. The prayers are honored as precious jewels. Purified and empowered, the words rise in a delightful fragrance to our Lord . . . your words do not stop until they reach the very throne of God.

～ Max Lucado
    The Great House of God

Pray to God but continue to row to the shore.

～ Russian Proverb

Bow, stubborn knees!

～ William Shakespeare
    Hamlet

Praying for Miracles

People who pray for miracles usually don't get miracles,
any more than children who pray for bicycles, good grades,
or boyfriends get them as a result of praying.
But people who pray for courage,
for strength to bear the unbearable,
for the grace to remember what they have left
instead of what they have lost,
very often find their prayers answered.
They discover that they have more strength, more courage
than they ever knew themselves to have.

    ~ Rabbi Harold S. Kushner
       When Bad Things Happen to Good People

One more prayer that is sure to be answered: often we beg
God to take care of the people we love. We do not need to.
God loves our loved ones more than we do.

    ~ Robert J. Cormier

Go bury thy sorrow,
  The world hath its share;
Go, bury it deeply,
  Go, hide it with care.
Go, bury thy sorrow,
  Let others be blest;
Go, give them the sunshine,
  And tell God the rest.

∼ Author Unknown

Abraham Lincoln claimed that reading the Bible was "the best cure for the blues." Many readers through the centuries have agreed with him. This is because the Bible, page after page, presents us with a loving, compassionate God who is always willing to aid those who turn to him. There is no problem, physical or mental, that is too small or too trivial to bring to God. This is the greatest comfort of all: The Ruler of the universe, the Almighty, lends his ear to us.

∼ J. Stephen Lang
  Biblical Quotations for All Occasions

When I learned that my friend Lynne's mother was dying of cancer, I didn't know how I could help. Since I didn't know her mother, I decided to purchase a certificate for a nice spa facial for Lynne, who was experiencing the stress of being the caretaker. On the card I wrote, "Perhaps this gift will allow you a little relaxation, so there'll be more of you to give to your mother."

— JENNIFER

Years before the discovery of antibiotics, the great behaviorist Ivan Pavlov lay dying of a widespread infection. He sent an assistant to the river with the odd task of bringing back a bucket of warm mud. That done, Pavlov stuck his hands in the bucket and began to play in the mud like a child. A few hours later his fever broke. He reasoned that if he could re-create the most peaceful, wonderful moment of his life, his body would have the maximal chance to heal. Remembering that his mother used to do her laundry in the river when he was a child, telling him stories as he played contentedly in the mud, he re-created that scene, and, sure enough, his body returned to inner balance.

Affirmation

Some
Heaven-sought answers
Come in sound—
A voice, perhaps.
But I have found
Mine always come
In utter silence.

My heart,
A swollen sea,
Stops tearing
At its shores
And gradually stills.
The whipping
Of the wind,
The gull's sharp cry—
All sounds
Cease.

I listen
To the answer.

Silence
Speaks clearly:
It speaks peace.

～ Carol Lynn Pearson

My husband was in the service and stationed overseas for ten months and I had a two- and a five-year-old at home. Friends would call occasionally to see how I was doing, but I was surprised and delighted when an anonymous friend hired a lawn service to take care of our front yard for more than six months. I never found out who it was, but it was a much appreciated gesture.

<small>∽ SHAWNDRA</small>

Many of the good people of the world pray. But the trouble with many of our prayers is that we give them as if we were picking up the telephone and ordering groceries—we place our order and hang up. We need to meditate, contemplate, think of what we are praying about and for, and then speak to the Lord as one person speaks to another. "Come now, and let us reason together, saith the Lord" (Isaiah 1:18). That is the invitation.

∽ Gordon B. Hinckley
  Standing for Something

Quietness

"Be still and know that I am God,"
That I who made and gave thee life
Will lead thy faltering steps aright;
That I who see each sparrow's fall
Will hear and heed thy earnest call.
I am God.

"Be still and know that I am God,"
When aching burdens crush thy heart,
Then know I form thee for thy part
And purpose in the plan I hold.
Trust in God.

"Be still and know that I am God,"
Who made the atom's tiny span
And set it moving to My plan,
That I who guide the stars above
Will guide and keep thee in My love.
Be thou still.

~ Doran

Raymond and the Bus

Some years ago our family's car broke down and the eight of us found ourselves stranded on a desolate stretch of highway in the middle of the Mojave desert, with July temperatures of about 110 to 120 degrees. Few cars passed and those that did sped by without slowing. The situation seemed serious, but we had not taken into account the faith of our three-year-old brother, Raymond.

Dad was trying to flag a car when Raymond said, "Don't worry, Dad. I'm gonna go talk with God and ask Him to send a bus to get us."

Raymond walked off, knelt down, and with his hand cupped to his ear, began to talk. He was on his knees for quite some time, but he finally got up, came over to us, and said, "Don't worry, Dad. Everything's gonna be all right now. God's gonna send a bus to get us." Raymond was firm in his declaration.

Within moments a bus materialized out of the heat waves and stopped. We watched, completely amazed, as my father asked the driver if he could take us to Las Vegas. The driver agreed and we boarded, filling the remaining seven seats. Dad remained with the car until we reached Las Vegas and called a relative who went to pick him up.

Afterward, when Dad spoke of the events of that blazing July day, he said that as the bus driver opened the door, he commented, "I don't know why I'm stopping. I'm hours behind schedule. It's company policy not to stop on the desert, but I just felt I should stop."

Raymond did not hear the driver's comment, but he already knew in his heart why the bus had stopped.

~ Kathleen Conger Ellis

We often ask, "What's wrong?" Doing so, we invite painful seeds of sorrow to come up and manifest. We feel suffering, anger, and depression, and produce more such seeds. We would be much happier if we tried to stay in touch with the healthy, joyful seeds inside of us and around us. We should learn to ask, "What's not wrong?" and be in touch with that. There are so many elements in the world and within our bodies, feelings, perceptions, and consciousness that are wholesome, refreshing, and healing. If we block ourselves, if we stay in the prison of our sorrow, we will not be in touch with these healing elements.

~ Thich Nhat Hanh
  Peace Is Every Step

The fruit of silence is prayer;
The fruit of prayer is faith;
The fruit of faith is love;
The fruit of love is service;
The fruit of service is peace.

~ On Mother Teresa's business card
The Joy in Loving

Wandering Prayer

Why, O Lord, is it so hard for me to keep my heart directed toward You? Why do the many little things I want to do, and the many people I know, keep crowding into my mind, even during the hours that I am totally free to be with You and You alone? Why does my mind wander off in so many directions, and why does my heart desire the things that lead me astray? Are You not enough for me? Do I keep doubting Your being, whether You will give me all I need if I just keep my eyes on You?

Please accept my distractions, my fatigue, my irritations, and my faithless wanderings. You know me more deeply and fully than I know myself. You love me with a greater love than I can love myself. You even offer me more than I can desire.

Look at me, see me in all my misery and inner confusion, and let me sense Your presence in the midst of my turmoil. All I can do is show myself to You. Yet, I am afraid to do so. I am afraid that You will reject me. But I know—with the knowledge of faith—that You desire to give me Your love. The only thing You ask of me is not to hide from You, not to run away in despair, not to act as if You were a relentless despot.

Take my tired body, my confused mind, and my restless soul into Your arms and give me rest, simple quiet rest. Do I ask too much too soon? I should not worry about that. You will let me know. Amen.

~ Henri J. Nouwen
  Treasury of Prayer

Drop thy still dews of quietness till all our striving cease;
    Take from our souls the strain and stress,
    And let our ordered lives confess
The beauty of thy Peace.

~ John Greenleaf Whittier

We have to fight them daily, like fleas, those many small worries about the morrow, for they sap our energies . . . The things that have to be done must be done, and for the rest we must not allow ourselves to become infested with thousands of petty fears and worries, so many motions of no confidence in God. Ultimately, we have just one moral duty: to reclaim large areas of peace in ourselves, more and more peace, and reflect it towards others. And the more peace there is in us, the more peace there will also be in our troubled world.

~ Ette Hillesum, written in her Nazi concentration camp diary
From *Sabbath* by Wayne Muller

When I get to heaven, I can sit and talk to God. I'll thank him first. It's always good to do more thanking than asking. It's one of the problems I have down here.

~ Paul Schoenfelder, age 7

Breathe in your blessings; breathe out your prayers.

~ Anonymous

God doesn't answer your prayers right after you ask. It takes awhile. Just like medicine. When you take it, it doesn't relieve you right away, it takes awhile for it to get in that place and dissolve in it. I don't know why He doesn't answer them right away. Trust me, if I knew, I would tell everyone.

~ Hannah Welch, age 11

Everybody should spend more time with God. Don't just talk to him on business.

~ Zachery Russell, age 8

Two years ago, I was laid off work. Being a single mom, I was naturally worried about finding a new job and taking care of the kids, and I became pretty depressed. One afternoon when I felt like no one in the world cared about me, there was a knock at the door. There stood my sister with a big box of "Cheer" detergent in her arms. Instead of soap, it was filled with my favorite cookies, a funny video, a joke book, a box of Cracker Jacks, a key-chain, and a juicy novel. Every time I looked at the box over the next few days, it helped me know someone cared.

∽ THERESA

Fear not, for I have redeemed you;
I have called you by name and you are mine.
When you pass through the waters, I will be with you;
And when you pass through the rivers, they shall not
    overwhelm you;
When you walk through fire you shall not be burned,
And the flames shall not consume you.
Because you are precious in my eyes, and honored,
And I love you.

∽ Isaiah 43:1b-2,4

Prayer at Gettysburg

The year 1863 was crucial not only for the outcome of the Civil War but ultimately for the future of the United States. The war had already raged for two years. The Emancipation Proclamation, declaring an end to slavery in the nation, had gone into effect in January. Later, President Lincoln set aside April 30 as a day of fasting, prayer and humility. But in early July, the Battle of Gettysburg began. The stakes were high, because this battle could well determine the outcome of the war.

Just before the battle began, President Lincoln prayed fervently, and he left a record of his appeal to God: "I went to my room one day and I locked the door and got down on my knees before Almighty God and prayed to Him mightily for victory at Gettysburg. I then and there made a solemn vow to Almighty God that if He would stand by our boys at Gettysburg, I would stand by Him. Soon a sweet comfort crept into my soul that God Almighty had taken the whole business into His own hands and that things would go all right at Gettysburg."

But not even Lincoln understood how powerfully God would answer his prayer. Colonel Joshua Chamberlain described the event in his report to the War Department:

"Our lines began to break before the overwhelming number of Rebel soldiers. Our guns let loose, but the enemy kept coming. We had to defend that hill. To lose Little Round Top would have been to lose everything.

"Then a terrible thing happened: we ran out of ammunition. I thought we would have to pull back. [Then] out of nowhere rode a tall figure on a shining white horse. Now I know this is incredible, but the rider was dressed as a Revolutionary general and the face—I will swear it was the face of George Washington! He raised his arm high and gave the signal to advance. My men began to shout and cheer. The Rebels saw it, too, and they began to shoot at it. The figure rode back and forth and the Confederate guns followed it. He should have been killed a thousand times over. No human being could have survived that fire. The rider urged our men on and raising their bayonets, they charged down the hill on top of the Rebels. The bayonet charge must have taken them by surprise for they turned and fled. We almost lost Little Round Top, and if we had, we could have lost Gettysburg."

∽ Author Unknown

When God doesn't do what we want, it's not easy. Never has been. Never will be. But faith is the conviction that God knows more than we do about this life and he will get us through it.

Remember, disappointment is caused by unmet expectations. Disappointment is cured by revamped expectations.

Next time you're disappointed, don't panic. Don't give up. Just be patient and let God remind you he's still in control. It ain't over till it's over.

～ Max Lucado
God's Inspirational Promise Book

Ah! If you only knew the peace there is in an accepted sorrow.

～ Jeanne de la Motte-Guyton

If you want to kiss the sky, you better learn how to kneel.

～ U2

Ian Gawler was a twenty-five-year-old veterinarian and decathlon athlete when his leg was amputated at the hip because of bone cancer. Within a few months, the cancer had metastasized throughout his body, and he was given two weeks to live. Instead of accepting the limitation of his prognosis, he married Grace, his veterinary nurse, and the two of them set about receiving healing on every level. They consulted energy healers and psychic healers. Ian changed his diet and spent hours each day in a form of deep, silent meditation similar to centering prayer. Over a period of four years, the cancer gradually disappeared. Twenty years later, my husband and I asked Ian to what he attributed his remarkable healing. He answered, "Peace of mind."

∽ Joan Borysenko, Ph.D.
Pocketful of Miracles

What Ties Me to the Earth Is Unseen

My heart was beating like a heron awakened
in the weeds, no room to move. Tangled
and surprised by the noise of my mind,
I fluttered without grace to the center
of the lake which humans call silence.

I guess, if you should ask, peace
is no more than the underside
of tired wings resting on the lake
while the heart in its feathers
pounds softer and softer.

~ Mark Nepo
     From *Sabbath* by Wayne Muller

On Waking in Prison

O God, early in the morning I cry to you.
Help me to pray
And to concentrate my thoughts on you:
I cannot do this alone.
In me there is darkness,
But with you there is light;
I am lonely, but you do not leave me;
I am feeble in heart, but with you there is help;
I am restless, but with you there is peace.
In me there is bitterness, but with you there is patience;
I do not understand your ways,
But you know the way for me . . .

～　Dietrich Bonhoeffer (1906–1945)
　　　Written while waiting execution in a Nazi prison

Be content with what you have;
　Rejoice in the way things are.
When you realize there is nothing lacking,
　The whole world belongs to you.

～　Lao-Tzu

How often we look upon God as our last and feeblest resource! We go to Him because we have nowhere else to go. And then we learn that the storms of life have driven us, not upon the rocks, but into the desired haven.

~ George Macdonald

Precious Lord, take my hand.
Lead me on. Let me stand.
I am tired. I am weak. I am worn.
Through the storm,
Through the night,
Lead me on to the light.
Take my hand, precious Lord,
and lead me home.

~ African American Spiritual

CHAPTER 5

Loss and Healing

"The soul would have no rainbow if the eyes had no tears."

JOHN PIPER

Your husband's job promotion has caused you to relocate to a new city and although it's a wonderful opportunity for him, you're missing your friends in your former hometown. Your sister-in-law just had a miscarriage—her third, and she can't even talk about it on the phone with you. Your father calls every week, and you sense his loneliness since your youngest brother left for college, leaving your parents' nest empty. You've just learned that your good friend from college has been diagnosed with multiple sclerosis. And your teenage son's tender heart has just been broken by a flighty and flirtatious girlfriend.

Each of these people has suffered a loss, and with any loss there is accompanying pain—the kind of bone-deep pain that every one of us will reckon with sooner or later in life. But this hallowing out of the heart we call loss can be a great teacher. It offers us a series of weanings, starting all the way back in infancy. Each loss pushes us toward realizing that the universe doesn't revolve around us and that life stretches out for miles in all directions. If we can open our eyes and see it, a fascinating world may be waiting for us, with new gifts and opportunities ready to fill the spaces left by our losses.

But how do we heal from losses that feel as real as if a limb had been cut off? How can we feel whole again when we so desperately miss that which is gone from our lives? Usually, it's a process that requires time—time to experience each natural stage in the grieving process.

Upon finishing his tremendous work on the French Revolution, Thomas Carlyle gave his manuscript to John Stuart Mill to read. By mistake, Mill's servant used the manuscript to start a fire. When Carlyle heard of this he fell into utter despair. Two years of hard work gone! He felt he could never rewrite it. Then one day he saw a mason building a wall—laying one brick at a time. Carlyle took new courage. He could rewrite his book—one page at a time.

Over time, and one step or one page at a time, people do heal. But to take the first step often requires someone to hold your hand, to encourage, comfort, and travel with you on your upward climb. When you are the one experiencing a loss, it's vitally important to seek help: counselors, clergy, and grief support groups are extremely valuable in offering guidance and solace. But besides reaching out, there are simple things you can do to help in your own recovery. Be good to yourself physically, maintain a lighter than usual daily routine, and try to live each day in the present. Allow yourself to cry without apologizing, expect to feel guilty and angry for a time, and know that these feelings will eventually subside. The healing process is a different journey for each person, and it follows no set time frame or pattern. So above all, be patient with yourself.

When someone close to you has suffered a loss—whether a death, a divorce, the loss of a job or the loss of a dream, take the time to explore what would help him or her most. More often than not, it won't be something that costs money but rather a gift of your time, a gift of yourself. Oprah Winfrey once said, "Lots of people want to ride with you in the limo, but what you want is someone who will take the bus with you when the limo breaks down." Be that person. It's not always convenient, but if you're willing to ride the bus with a friend in need, someday someone will show up for you—just when you're most in need of a lift.

I cannot remove the pain of death or bring a loved one
back to life.

I cannot explain God's plan or even pretend to understand.

I cannot tell you that your loved one has gone to a happier
place, without knowing it now makes the earth the
saddest place.

But, my dear friend, I can tell you that there is a time you
will heal and the devastating pain won't always be so real.

I can weep with you when you weep and stay to dry the
tears when you can't sleep.

I can tell you that your loved one fought the fight and kept
his faith and now it is your turn to finish the race.

∽ Dianne Waggoner
  In *A Gift of Mourning Glories* by Georgia Shaffer

When it is dark enough, you can see the stars.

∽ Ralph Waldo Emerson

The Christmas after I got laid off was meager for our family. Although we still had a roof over our heads, there was almost no cash to buy gifts, let alone food for the holidays. I remember walking outside to a blustery snowstorm a few days before Christmas, only to find an envelope on our front porch with $150 inside from an anonymous source. We never knew who it came from, but I will always remember watching our kids open each cherished gift. Our family was grateful that day not only for gifts of love, but for the warmth and comfort of being able to pay the overdue heating bill.

~ VLAD

When we walk to the edge of all the light we have and we take a step into the darkness of the unknown, we must believe one of two things will happen—there will be something solid to stand on, or we will be taught to fly.

~ Martin Edges

In this sad world of ours, sorrow comes to all . . . It comes
   with bittersweet agony . . .
Perfect relief is not possible, except with time.
You cannot now realize that you will ever feel better . . .
And yet this is a mistake. You are sure to be happy again,
   to know this, which is surely true,
Will make you seem less miserable now.
I have experienced enough to know what I say.

~ Abraham Lincoln
   (Three of Abraham Lincoln's sons died: Edward, age 4;
   William, age 11; and Thomas, age 18.)

The melody that the loved one played upon the piano of
your life will never be played quite that way again, but we
must not close the keyboard and allow the instrument to
gather dust. We must seek out other artists of the spirit,
new friends who gradually will help us to find the road to
life again, who will walk that road with us.

~ Rabbi Joshua Liebman
   Peace of Mind

Every loss needs a hundred tellings.

~ Anonymous

Who never mourned hath never known
  What treasures grief reveals,
The sympathies that humanize,
  The tenderness that heals.

~ Author Unknown

Believe me, every heart has its secret sorrow,
Which the world knows not;
And oftentimes we call a man cold
When he is only sad.

~ Henry Wadsworth Longfellow

In a story called "The Turn of the Tide," Arthur Gordon tells of a time in his life when he began to feel that everything was stale and flat. His enthusiasm waned; his writing efforts were fruitless. And the situation was growing worse day by day.

Finally, he determined to get help from a medical doctor. Observing nothing physically wrong, the doctor asked him if he would be able to follow his instructions for one day.

When Gordon replied that he could, the doctor told him to spend the following day in the place where he was happiest as a child. He could take food, but he was not to talk to anyone or to read or write or listen to the radio. He then wrote out four prescriptions and told him to open one at nine, at twelve, three, and six o'clock.

"Are you serious?" Gordon asked him.

"You won't think I'm joking when you get my bill!" was the reply.

So the next morning, Gordon went to the beach. As he opened the first prescription, he read "Listen carefully." He thought the doctor was insane. How could he listen for three hours? But he had agreed to follow the doctor's orders, so he listened. He heard the usual sounds of the sea and the birds. After a while, he could hear the other sounds that weren't so apparent at first. As he listened, he began to think of lessons the sea had taught him as a child— patience, respect, an awareness of the interdependence of things. He began to listen to the sounds—and the silence—and to feel a growing peace.

At noon, he opened the second slip of paper and read "Try reaching back." "Reaching back to what?" he wondered. Perhaps to childhood, perhaps to memories of happy times. He thought about his past, about the many little moments of joy. He tried to remember them with exactness. And in remembering, he found a growing warmth inside.

At three o'clock, he opened the third piece of paper. Until now, the prescriptions had been easy to take. But this one was different; it said "Examine your motives." At first he was defensive. He thought about what he wanted—success, recognition, security—and he justified them all. But then the thought occurred to him that those motives weren't good enough, and that perhaps therein was the answer to his stagnant situation.

He considered his motives deeply. He thought about past happiness. And at last, the answer came to him.

"In a flash of certainty," he wrote, "I saw that if one's motives are wrong, nothing can be right. It makes no difference whether you are a mailman, a hairdresser, an insurance salesman, a housewife—whatever. As long as you feel you are serving others, you do the job well. When you are concerned only with helping yourself, you do it less well—a law as inexorable as gravity."

When six o'clock came, the final prescription didn't take long to fill. "Write your worries on the sand," it said. He knelt and wrote several words with a piece of broken shell; then he turned and walked away. He didn't look back; he knew the tide would come in.

~ Stephen R. Covey
  The 7 Habits of Highly Effective People

Dearest Mother and Father God, my despair feels like a tangible force, so engulfing that it encompasses my thoughts. Knowing this and in the acceptance of it, allow me to ride it through and come out on the other side, brighter and unscathed.

I realize that reaching the depths of my soul's sorrow is a ferocious lesson, but I will, with your mighty sword, triumph over my pain, loss, and suffering. I will see your golden sword cut through the cobwebs of my mind and bring light to my desert. Amen.

~ Sylvia Browne
  Prayers

After my young son died, I was in shock and was paralyzed by my grief. A good friend went out and bought some cards and then helped address, stamp, and mail the acknowledgments and thank-yous to all those people who had helped with the funeral and had sent flowers. I never could've done it on my own.

∼ MARIA

We do not succeed in changing things according to our desire, but gradually our desire changes. The situation that we hoped to change because it was intolerable becomes unimportant. We have not managed to surmount the obstacle, as we were absolutely determined to do, but life has taken us round it, led us past it, and then if we turn round to gaze at the remote past, we can barely catch sight of it, so imperceptible has it become.

∼ Marcel Proust

A Prayer for Animals

Hear our humble prayer, O God,
For our friends, the animals,
Especially for those who are suffering;
For any that are lost or deserted
Or frightened or hungry.

We entreat for them all Thy mercy and pity,
And for those who deal with them,
We ask a heart of compassion
And gentle hands and kindly words.
Make us, ourselves,
To be true friends to animals
And so to share
The blessings of the merciful.

~ Albert Schweitzer

Tearless grief bleeds inwardly.

~ C. N. Bovee

After I was divorced, it was difficult to attend social gatherings alone and I noticed I didn't get invited to "couples" events as much. One friend and her husband decided to have a "Three's Company" night once a month, including me (or other singles) in their weekend outing—to a movie, restaurant, play, or family picnic.

                                             ⟶ MAI

The best thing about the future is that it only comes one day at a time.

⟶ Abraham Lincoln

The head does not know how to play the part of the heart for long.

⟶ La Rochefoucauld

Prayer Reading for Healing

It is true. I stand at the door of your heart, day and night. Even when you are not listening, even when you doubt it could be Me, I am there. I await even the smallest sign of your response, even the least whispered invitation that will allow Me to enter. And always, without fail, with infinite power and love, bringing the many gifts of My Spirit. I come with My mercy, with My desire to forgive and heal you, and with a love for you beyond your comprehension.

I come longing to console you and give you strength, to lift you up and bind your wounds . . . Come to me with your misery, with your troubles and needs, and with all your longing to be loved. I stand at the door of your heart and knock.

~ Ron Roth, Ph.D.
The Healing Path of Prayer

I am a more sensitive person, a more effective pastor, a more sympathetic counselor because of my son Aaron's life and death than I would ever have been without it. And I would give up all of those gains in a second if I could have my son back. If I could choose, I would forego all the spiritual growth and depth which has come my way because of our experiences, and be what I was fifteen years ago, an average rabbi, an indifferent counselor, helping some people and unable to help others, and the father of a bright, happy boy. But I cannot choose.

~ Rabbi Harold S. Kushner
When Bad Things Happen to Good People

I wish there were some wonderful place
Called the Land of Beginning Again,
Where all our mistakes and all our heartaches
And all our poor selfish grief
Could be dropped, like a shabby old coat at the door
And never put on again.

~ Louisa Fletcher Tarkington

There is an old Tibetan tale about a young woman, Krisha Gotami, who gave birth to a much-loved son. When her firstborn was a year old, he fell ill and died. Grief-stricken, Krisha Gotami walked through her city, holding the small body in her arms, begging for medicine to bring the child back to life. Some people ignored her; others laughed at her. Still others thought she was mad. Finally she came to a wise man who told her the only person on Earth who could help her was Buddha. She went to Buddha and recounted her tale. He listened carefully, then told Krisha Gotami he would help her if she would go into the city and bring him a mustard seed from the first home she came to that had not known death.

Elated, Krisha Gotami ran to the city and knocked on the door of the first house she encountered. "Buddha has sent me to retrieve a mustard seed from a house that has never known death," she said. "This is not a good house," said the owner. "We have known death here." She went to the next house and was told the same, and on to the next, and the next, until she had knocked on the door of every house in the city and remained unable to fulfill Buddha's request.

Having learned about the universality of suffering, she was able to bury her child, bid him farewell, and tell Buddha, "I understand what you were trying to teach me. I was too blinded by my own grief to see that we all suffer."

～ Buddhist tale retold by Susan Zimmermann
   Writing to Heal the Soul

The Rainy Day

The day is cold and dark and dreary;
It rains, and the wind is never weary;
The vine still clings to the moldering wall,
But at every gust the dead leaves fall,
  And the day is dark and dreary.

My life is cold and dark and dreary;
It rains, and the wind is never weary;
My thoughts still cling to the moldering past,
But the hopes of youth fall thick in the blast,
  And the days are dark and dreary.

Be still, sad heart! And cease repining;
Behind the clouds is the sun still shining:
Thy fate is the common fate of all:
Into each life some rain must fall,
  Some days must be dark and dreary.

~ Henry Wadsworth Longfellow

Little Boy Blue

The little toy dog is covered with dust,
But sturdy and staunch he stands;
And the little toy soldier is red with rust,
And his musket moulds in his hands.
Time was when the little toy dog was new,
And the soldier was passing fair;
And that was the time when our Little Boy Blue
Kissed them and put them there.

"Now, don't you go till I come," he said,
"And don't you make any noise!"
So, toddling off to his trundle-bed,
He dreamt of the pretty toys;
And, as he was dreaming, an angel song
Awakened our Little Boy Blue—
Oh! The years are many, the years are long,
But the little toy friends are true!

Ay, faithful to Little Boy Blue they stand,
Each in the same old place,
Awaiting the touch of a little hand,
The smile of a little face;
And they wonder, as waiting the long years through
In the dust of that little chair,
What has become of our Little Boy Blue,
Since he kissed them and put them there.

⁓ Eugene Field

Although the world is full of suffering, it is full also of the overcoming of it.

⁓ Helen Keller

Three words were in the captain's heart. He shaped them soundlessly with his trembling lips, as he had not breath to spare for a whisper: "I am lost." And having given up life, the Captain suddenly began to live.

~ Carson McCullers

Earth has no sorrow that Heaven cannot heal.

~ Thomas Moore

Dandelions

All night we watched from our window as waves of fire curled and broke over the hills around our valley in California and formed in crooked lines into the dark. A combination of fear and fascination kept us watching as the flames fed on grasses that eddied and billowed in the constant wind like sheets on a clothesline. The crests of the blaze surged and fountained against clumps of chaparral, laced among yucca, sage, and scrub oak, and reached for houses firemen were trying to fence from the bright tide with slender wires of water.

It was gloriously beautiful for a few hours, but in the morning the hills were charred carcasses with rocky bones sticking through. I grieved over the remains until someone told me that these fiery floods every few years dissolve old wood into fertilizer and cause seeds that have waited dormant, impervious to rain and sun, to germinate. Searing signals them to sprout.

The seed in me has waited eighty-seven years for the old wood to blaze. Tiny fires burn silent in my cells, slow flames called carcinoma. I'm glad I'm dying.

I've waited for death as I used to wait pregnant for labor to start. By the end of nine months, I felt so heavy, lame, and bloated, the body I'd lent was so busy and abused, I'd be willing to face anything to have it back again. "Did anyone ever just pop open?" I asked the doctor. He thought I was afraid, but I just wanted to know.

I wanted, too, to know about the cancer, but he offered empty words and pain killers.

Why does he hide the miracle of what is happening to me? Many times I've marveled in my morning mirror as time molded and mined my face and veined my hair with gray. I've often sighed in my evening prayers, "I'm glad I don't have to live this day over again," but I wouldn't have traded it for rubies.

Waiting is the hardest part. When I was pregnant, time would swell and stretch like my stomach, growing taut, until—well, I didn't pop, after all. Something silently switched on the ignition. Beyond my willing, contractions slowly gripped and eased, gradually accelerating the pace and pressure as if I were part of a machine going automatically through the cycles. The constant now of pain erased past and future, and I forgot what I was suffering for as the grinding pulse consumed existence until everything but pain was shadow.

Hardly anyone nowadays has a baby at home. I had three before they made me hurry to the hospital to let the doctor catch the baby in orthodox fashion after I'd done the labor. "Twilight sleep," they offered, once, to dull the pain, but I wouldn't let them rob me. I'd rather earn the joy of seeing the child's wet triumph, hearing the angry yowling. The victory was in letting the mechanism use me until I could use it. I didn't even need the doctor for six babies. But Eddy wedged sideways.

"I think I've broken his arm," the doctor said.

"I can't. I can't do it!" I was helpless with terror.

"You can," he said. And I did. "Here's just a little problem with club feet, but an operation will take care of that," he cheered me.

I lived through that time and others when it seemed I could not live. Even when Eddy died. In the long wait while he withered, we picked armfuls of laughter, even in the living tomb of the hospital. We put goldfish in the water pitcher and held a wheelchair rodeo in the hall.

We giggled until even the giggle was gone. I wanted to die too. No, not to die, to cease to exist. I wanted to dissolve. Eddy had been woven into the fabric of my life, and when death tore him out, it left a raveled web, impossible to patch or darn. I knew he was safe, but my heart wanted a letter from him that I could fold and keep in my pocket.

After he was buried, I would think about him in heaven, wonder whether he was behaving, saying, "Yes, Sir," to the Lord, still eleven years old to me, even though I knew he wasn't a boy there. Even now the healed-over hurt is lumpy and touch-tender. Eddy's image, faded with the bleach and suds of many Mondays, keeps coming to the surface like a nail under the linoleum.

I couldn't heal, couldn't grow back together when Dan died because a knife had neatly sliced me in half. For fifty-three years we were like the thumb and first finger on a hand. At first we dropped a few things, but we gradually learned to turn the pages and pick up pins.

My hair has puffed into sparse white fluff now, but then—a spring-silly race across the pasture, lifting my long skirts a bit to leap across the irrigation ditch, and my carefully combed and pinned-up hairdo collapsed in a cascade of brown floss. I knelt breathless on the edge of the stream, harvesting hairpins and trying to make a mirror of the water that ran between us.

Dan laughed at me in great gusts.

"You fix it, then," I snapped, knowing that each vinegar-rinsed strand caught fire in the sunlight.

He knelt and washed his hands and wrists in it. "The most beautiful hair I've ever seen," he said, leaning across the running water to kiss me, in broad daylight, with the sun falling heavy on us and spreading itself out in a pond of dandelions.

The yellow flowers we made wreaths of went to weeds when Dan turned that pasture for a truck garden. We planted our marriage and our first son with the parsnips and pumpkins. Dandelions will cheer an empty lot or make a spring salad; we put them in our root beer and tonics; but they're the dickens to get out of the garden. If you hack them off too short, they grow back, and if you let even one fuzzy button sneak up next to a tomato plant, the wind will scatter silky parachutes to grow and hoe for years to come.

Between the rows of potatoes, Polly slowly unbent her back and leaned on her hoe to ask, "Mama, how does it feel to fall in love?"

"I don't know. Between planting and harvesting, there's a lot of work to be done. It's easy to plant, but you'd better want to plow and prune with someone when you let yourself love. Your father and I didn't fall in it; we grew it." Like an apple tree—with a bumper crop every other year. And I nursed, half dozing, in the night.

Irrigated with laughter, love grew tall and green on composted sorrow and hard times. It was more good than bad, but I'm glad I'll never have to hoe weeds again. No more canker sores, flies in the house, plucking and gutting chickens, prying frozen stiff overalls off the line with numb fingers, and watching when I switch on the light in the cellar for the scuttle of roaches to tell me to put out poison. Dan's snoring used to bother me, too, but I learned to sleep through it. "I don't snore; I just sleep loud," he'd tell us.

The night the snoring stopped, I called the doctor, but I knew the net of tubes and tapes they put him in wouldn't hold him long. Just long enough for sons to circle him, and daughters to reflect his radiance in their tears. Dan performed his dying with enjoyment, an Abraham bestowing blessings on the bouquet gathered from his scattered seed.

"Shall I treat him like a young man?" the doctor asked.

"And make a mere rehearsal of his death?" I cried. "He'd never forgive you."

Eddy had to struggle out of life like a chick from its shell, but Dan's flame went out in a gentle puff. And now it's my turn.

This soul has kicked and bumped inside me all my life, and now when I'd like to hurry to heaven and let the Lord catch my spirit, it's wedged sideways. In this, my last labor, Lord, deliver me!

∽ Penny Allen

Every Life Is Cherished

The earth will never be the same again.
Rock, water, tree, iron, share this grief
As distant stars participate in pain,
A candle snuffed, a falling star or leaf,
A dolphin death, O this particular loss
Is Heaven-mourned; for if no angel cried,
If this small one was tossed away as dross,
The very galaxies then would have lied.
How shall we sing our love's song now
In this strange land where all are born to die?
Each tree and leaf and star show how
The universe is part of their one cry,
That every life is noted and is cherished,
And nothing loved is ever lost or perished.

∽ Madeleine L'Engle
Glimpses of Grace

∽

My good friend was dying at age 37 and leaving a 12-year-old daughter and 10-year-old son behind. I took her shopping one day in her wheelchair to pick out just the perfect wedding present for each of her children. She wrote special wedding cards to each and I helped her wrap them so that many years from then, they both would feel their mother's presence on their joyful day.

∼ TENIELLE

There are many trials in life which do not seem to come from unwisdom or folly; they are silver arrows shot from the bow of God, and fixed inextricably in the quivering heart—they are meant to be borne—they were not meant, like snow or water, to melt as soon as they strike; but the moment an ill can be patiently borne it is disarmed of its poison, though not of its pain.

∼ Henry Ward Beecher

CHAPTER 6

The Promise of Immortality

"The only way to take the sorrow out of death is to
take love out of life."

AUTHOR UNKNOWN

fter forty years of service in Africa as a Christian
missionary, Henry C. Morrison headed home by
boat. Theodore Roosevelt was also aboard that
same boat. Morrison was quite dejected when, upon enter-
ing New York harbor, the president received a great fanfare
as he arrived on his home shore. Morrison thought he should
get some recognition for his forty years in the Lord's service.
Then a small voice came to Morrison: Henry, you're not
home yet.

Going home. That's how some people view what happens
to them when they die. In fact, most people believe they

will exist in some other realm or afterlife, returning "home" to join friends and family who have already passed away. In her popular '70s song, singer Peggy Lee posed the question "Is That All There Is?" When applied to our mortal existence, the answer for most people is still a resounding "No!" C. S. Lewis tells us, "Nature is mortal. We shall outlive her. When all the suns and nebulae have passed away, each one of you will still be alive." When dealing with the death of a friend or loved one, a belief in the promise of immortality is a tremendous source of strength and comfort.

But regardless of what one believes about the hereafter, facing mortality—your own or a loved one's—is still extremely difficult. Whatever the circumstances—a death due to Alzheimer's disease in an eighty-year-old woman, the death of a young child from a car accident, or even the death of the family dog, those left behind will feel sorrow, grief, often shock and denial, and sometimes anger and guilt for a period of time. In every case, those who are suffering need to be encircled in the arms of love and given the permission to grieve.

Unfortunately, many people feel inadequate when it comes to knowing what to say or do for someone who is grieving. Too often, we feel awkward, embarrassed, afraid we'll cause more pain if we say something, so we stay away or say nothing. This book provides simple tools for knowing what and what not to say, as well as specific words of comfort for those in need. But the underlying message is this: it is always better to say something or do something than do nothing at all.

Louise Carroll writes in *Be a Comfort* about the way a grief-stricken person will normally react to those who show support and offer hope, even when done awkwardly or imperfectly: "Through his tears he may not see clearly, but his heart will be warmed by the human touch and loving care. Later, he may not remember what was said, but he will remember the warmth and closeness. He will remember there were those who cared. Over his sadness will be a mist of love, and it will help him through his difficult time."

Life is terminal—we all die sooner or later. But the great promise of immortality is that although the loss of a spouse, child, parent, or beloved friend seems unbearable at the moment, it is not the end. That person lives on in another realm, and will one day embrace those he left behind at his death.

Do not stand at my grave and weep;
I am not here, I do not sleep.
I am a thousand winds that blow;
I am the diamond glints on snow.
I am the sunlight on ripened grain;
I am the gentle autumn's rain.
When you awaken in the morning's hush,
I am the swift uplifting rush
Of quiet birds in circled flight.
I am the soft starlight at night.
Do not stand at my grave and cry,
I am not here, I did not die.

~ Author Unknown

To a Dying Father

You have grown wings of pain
And flap around the bed like a wounded gull
Calling for water, calling for tea, for grapes
Whose skins you cannot penetrate.
Remember when you taught me
How to swim? Let go, you said,
The lake will hold you up.
I long to say, Father let go
And death will hold you up . . .

~ Judith Viorst
   Necessary Losses

Life is real! Life is earnest!
And the grave is not its goal;
Dust thou art, to dust returnest,
Was not spoken of the soul.

~ Henry Wadsworth Longfellow

A few nights before Christmas one year, a drunk driver ran his car up on our lawn and crashed through the front bay window of our house, destroying everything in its path including our beautifully decorated Christmas tree. A few nights later, I heard carolers at the front door, and when we opened it, there were dozens of people from church, each handing us a brand-new Christmas ornament as they sang.

— JANIS

Benjamin Franklin wrote his own epitaph:

The body of Benjamin Franklin
(like the cover of an old book, its contents torn out, and
   stript of its lettering and gilding) lies here, food for
   worms.
Yet the work itself shall not be lost, for it will (as he
   believed)
appear once more, in a new and more beautiful edition,
corrected and amended by the author.

Heaven

When I was a boy I used to think of Heaven as a glorious golden city, with jeweled walls, and gates of pearl, with nobody in it but the angels, and they were all strangers to me. But after a while my little brother died; then I thought of Heaven as that great city, full of angels, with just one little fellow in it that I was acquainted with. He was the only one I knew there at that time.

Then another brother died, and there were two in Heaven that I knew. Then my acquaintances began to die, and the number of my friends in Heaven grew larger all the time. But, it was not till one of my own little ones was taken that I began to feel that I had a personal interest in Heaven.

Then a second went, and a third, and a fourth; and so many of my friends and loved ones have gone there, that it seems as if I know more in Heaven than I know on earth.

And now, when my thoughts turn to Heaven, it is not the gold and the jewels and the pearls that I think of—but the loved ones there. It is not the place so much as the company that makes Heaven seem beautiful.

~ Author Unknown

She always leaned to watch for us,
  Anxious if we were late,
In winter by the window,
  In summer by the gate;

And though we mocked her tenderly,
  Who had such foolish care,
The long way home would seem more safe
  Because she waited there.

Her thoughts were all so full of us,
  She never could forget!
And so I think that where she is
  She must be watching yet,

Waiting till we come home to her,
  Anxious if we are late—
Watching from Heaven's window,
  Leaning from Heaven's gate.

~ Margaret Widdemer
    Cross Currents

At the core of our being, rooted deep within our soul there is the knowing that we are indestructible. We have the hope of immortality, of life after death, which is an incentive for moral perfection. This inner knowing is hope and it is a stepping stone to the awakening of the soul. It is that still, but restless voice inside you that beckons you to a higher/faster energy. In a sense, hope is the restoration of the appetite for life itself.

∼ Wayne W. Dyer
There's a Spiritual Solution to Every Problem

Each departed friend is a magnet that attracts us to the next world.

∼ Jean Paul Richter

My father died when I was 14, and a few months later, an aunt made each of us kids a quilt. She made them out of my father's old flannel shirts and told us that when we missed him most, we could wrap ourselves in the quilt and pretend it was his loving arms around us. I've treasured my quilt ever since.

↬ RICHARD

I know you're fighters. I'm going to be watching over you, because I do believe there is a God. I want you to know that I'll be somewhere, still thinking about you and loving you and waiting for you . . .

I don't ever want to say good-bye, ever. And I don't think I'm going to because I'm going to see you again.

Brent, Blair, Blaine. When you feel like you should be holding me, hold your mother. It will be like you're hugging me, because she's half of me.

↬ Bonnie Remsberg
from the last videotape left by her husband before he died

I don't know which is wearier,
My body or my spirit.
The disease eats at my bones,
The medicines wipe me out.
But missing you
Is the heavier burden.
When I feel that my pains are your will,
Something you want to redeem
They are not hard to carry.
When I find in them no sense,
They seem only destructive.
I want to cry out in frustration
For all the wrong in the world.
We are small people, God,
As easily rolled up and crushed as paper.
The longest of our lives
Does not last one of your seconds.
Hold us close then in your meaning
Lest we feel terribly badly made.
Help us to believe
Deep in our souls
That you have purposes for our dying
And you let nothing decent be lost.

~ John Tully Carmody

God Is No Illusion: Meditations of the End of Life "Poem No. 24"

~

From Ode: Imitations of Immortality

Our birth is but a sleep and a forgetting;
The Soul that rises with us, our life's Star,
　　Hath had elsewhere its setting,
　　　　And cometh from afar:
　　Not in entire forgetfulness,
　　And not in utter nakedness,
But trailing clouds of glory do we come
　　From God, who is our home:
Heaven lies about us in our infancy!

～　William Wordsworth

Give sorrow words: the grief that does not speak, whispers in
the over-wrought heart and bids it break.

～　William Shakespeare

The House Dog's Grave

I've changed my ways a little; I cannot now
Run with you in the evenings along the shore,
Except in a kind of dream; and you, if you dream a
   moment,
You see me there.

So leave awhile the paw-marks on the front door
Where I used to scratch to go out or in,
And you'd soon open; leave on the kitchen floor
The marks of my drinking-pan.

I cannot lie by your fire as I used to do
On the warm stone,
Nor at the foot of your bed; no, all the night through
I lie alone.

But your kind thought has laid me less than six feet
Outside your window where firelight so often plays,
And where you sit to read—and I fear often
   grieving for me—
Every night your lamplight lies on my place.

You, man and woman, live so long, it is hard
To think of you ever dying
A little dog would get tired, living so long.
I hope that when you are lying

Under the ground like me your lives will appear
As good and joyful as mine.
No, dear, that's too much hope: you are not
    so well cared for
As I have been.

And never have known the passionate undivided
Fidelities that I knew.
Your minds are perhaps too active, too many-sided . . .
But to me you were true.

You were never masters, but friends. I was your friend.
I loved you well, and was loved. Deep love endures
To the end and far past the end. If this is my end,
I am not lonely. I am not afraid. I am still yours.

~ Robinson Jeffers

At the funeral of a close friend, I heard the following story and have never forgotten it.

In a beautiful blue lagoon on a clear day, a fine sailing-ship spreads its brilliant white canvas in a fresh morning breeze and sails out to the open sea. We watch her glide away magnificently through the deep blue and gradually see her grow smaller and smaller as she nears the horizon. Finally, where the sea and sky meet, she slips silently from sight; and someone near me says, "There, she is gone!"

Gone where? Gone from sight—that is all. She is still as large in mast and hull and sail, still just as able to bear her load. And we can be sure that, just as we say, "There she is gone!" another says, "There, she comes!"

~ Paul H. Dunn
   The Birth That We Call Death

When our family dog, Coco, died, we prepared a box for him to be buried in. The children helped line the inside of the box with their favorite pictures of themselves with Coco over the 10 years he'd been part of our family. We added his collar and his favorite toys to the box and then each child wrote a special note to the dog, expressing their love and sadness. It was a big part of the healing process over losing our family pet.

↪ SCOTT

A man had a very serious automobile accident that involved a long-term recovery. Contemplating his death—a real possibility for a while—he told his wife that he wanted only one word on his tombstone. That was *Vacant*. What an epitaph for a tombstone. It would have been precisely accurate: if he had died, he would not have occupied the grave. His body would have, but not he.

↪ R. Kent Hughes
   1001 Great Stories

Roadside Meetings

A little more tired at close of day,
A little less anxious to have our way;
A little less ready to scold and blame;
A little more care for a brother's name—
And so we are nearing the journey's end,
Where time and eternity meet and blend.
The book is closed and the prayers are said,
And we are a part of the countless dead.
Thrice happy then if some soul can say
"I live because he has passed this way."

~ Stephen Crane

We see but dimly through the mists and vapors;
Amid these earthly damps
What seem to us but sad funeral tapers,
May be heaven's distant lamps.

~ Author Unknown

Death is not extinguishing the light; it is putting out the lamp because the dawn has come.

～ Rabindranath Tagore

I feel and know that death is not the ending, as we thought, but rather the real beginning—and that nothing ever is or can be lost, nor even die, nor soul, nor matter.

～ Walt Whitman

This life is the crossing of a sea, where we meet in the same narrow ship. In death we reach the shore and go to our different worlds.

～ Rabindranath Tagore
Stray Birds

Love never disappears for death is a non-event.
I have merely retired to the room next door.
You and I are the same; what we were for each other,
   we still are.
Speak to me as you always have, do not use a different tone,
   do not be sad.
Continue to laugh at what made us laugh.
Smile and think of me.
Life means what it has always meant.
The link is not severed.
Why should I be out of your soul if I am out of your sight?
I will wait for you, I am not here, but just on the other side
   of this path.
You see, all is well.

~~ St. Augustine

Something has spoken to me in the night
Burning the tapers of the waning year,
Something has spoken in the night,
And told me I shall die,
I know not where.
Saying: "To lose the earth you know, for greater knowing,
To lose the life you have, for greater life,
To leave the friends you loved, for greater loving,
To find a land more kind than home, more large than earth
Whereon the pillars of this earth are founded,
Toward which the conscience of the world is tending—
A wind is rising, and the rivers flow."

∽ Thomas Wolfe
  You Can't Go Home Again

Our creator would never have made such lovely days, and
have given us the deep hearts to enjoy them, above and
beyond all thought, unless we were meant to be immortal.

∽ Nathaniel Hawthorne

Be like a bird
That pausing in her flight
A while on boughs to light,
Feels them give way
Beneath her and yet sings,
Knowing that she hath wings.

∽ Victor Hugo

I am ready to meet my Maker, but whether my Maker is prepared for the great ordeal of meeting me is another matter.

∽ Winston Churchill

CHAPTER 7

Faith, Hope, and Courage

"The best way out is always through."

ROBERT FROST

*I*n any year, on any day, we find ourselves worrying about much that has happened, hasn't happened, or doesn't happen. Problems, disappointments, and sorrow all lead to the same pervasive thought: What am I going to do now? And inevitably the answer is, continue to do what needs to be done, do what can be done, and have faith that life will unfold as it always has. "Where one door shuts, another opens" we are assured—but the challenge is finding the courage to move through the open door and face whatever's on the other side.

"Be not faint-hearted in misfortune," a wise person said and then added, "When God causes a tree to be hewn down He takes care that His birds can nestle on another." The pure innocence reflected in that statement might cause us to think it came from the lips of a child, and there are certainly times when a simple, unquestioning, childlike faith would come in handy. But life is complicated; we've been disappointed before, even heartbroken. Where can we find the peace or hope or childlike faith in such an uncertain world?

True, we live in precarious times and our country has been staggered by grievous losses in recent times. But we've also witnessed an amazing process of digging in, digging out, and pulling together—all performed with a kind of strength and courage we didn't know we had. The week after September 11, 2001, The Rev. Mary F. Harvey of St. Louis said to her congregation, "May we learn that courage is not the absence of fear, but the capacity to act in the presence of fear. Faith is not the absence of doubt, but the courage to believe in spite of doubt. Trust is not the absence of qualms, but the capacity to go forward despite misgivings."

Yes, the world has learned a thing or two about faith, hope, and courage in the new millennium. We've always had heroes to look to in other times and places, but now we are learning that common people in everyday settings—our neighbors and friends—have the same resilience and strength of spirit as the nobles, patriots, and pioneers in our history books.

My roommate in college came from a large family who struggled financially. Somehow, the parents managed to get her and her sister home to Oregon (from Utah) for the Christmas holidays, but a few months later, their 14-year-old sister was killed in a car accident. My roommate wanted to go home for the funeral but no one had the money. So I went knocking door-to-door throughout the dorms, explaining the situation, and everyone gladly chipped in. Even though college students are typically poor, after only one day of collecting, we handed my roommate a card signed by many of her friends and $600 inside—enough for both sisters to fly home.

~ OLIVIA

Winston Churchill, who rallied the Allies during World War II, was not only a hero, he was a meticulously organized man. He attended to all the details in his life—even his funeral, which he planned well ahead of its occurrence. Favorite scripture, beloved hymns, preferred readings were described and itemized. Author Andrea Cornett tells us that upon his death, Churchill's instructions were followed precisely. But funeral attendees sat astonished when the service concluded with not just one bugler, stationed high in the dome of St. Paul's Cathedral, but a second. The first played the traditional and somber taps. Across the dome, however, and in perfect counterpoint, the second bugler played the spirited notes of reveille. The message was clear: Get up. Begin a new day.

When a friend or family member is discouraged or has lost hope because of life's difficulties, we need to stand by patiently, lending an ear, offering a hug, giving reassurance that they will survive their current situation. True friends are those who listen not only with their ears, but with their hearts—acting as a sounding board as the person talks about their pain and their problems over and over. Listening in this way enables the discouraged person to begin making decisions, which is often a step on the road to hope and healing. With the support of those who love and care, even the most distraught person will eventually have the courage to "get up and begin a new day."

And how do you find faith, hope, and courage when you are the one who has lost it? The first thing to remember is that you are not alone. Most people experience periods of depression, when feelings of loneliness and isolation stir up dark clouds that seem fixed and immovable. At times like this, it is almost impossible to believe that anyone else has experienced the same degree of pain or that the feelings of despair will ever leave. Universal experience teaches us, however, that the dark clouds of depression do roll away eventually, and sometimes all at once. There are a few things you can do to help diffuse them sooner rather than later.

First, allow others to help you. Don't be afraid or embarrassed to tell a trusted friend or relative about your depression—you might be surprised by how willingly they'll come to the rescue with comfort and strength. If nothing else, talking about your feelings will release some frustration and help lift you out of the deep, dark, downward spiral of despair.

Some people find that expressing their feelings in writing is therapeutic. A journal can be a tool for relieving stress and sadness and a way to document your journey upward. Allowing yourself to cry is important, too. Crying is not a sign of weakness—it is a release mechanism that serves to lessen the pain. Essentially, crying is one of the most natural and accessible "self-help" tools around.

Most important, remember to live one day at a time. Try to take one step forward each day instead of trying to solve all your problems at once. Setting small, accomplishable goals will help restore your confidence and nourish you emotionally.

As the suffocating clouds of hopelessness begin to break up, you'll begin to notice brief moments when narrow rays of sunshine slice boldly through the grayness of your life. Though you may continue to struggle, holding onto that new hope will brighten your outlook and allow you to cope more effectively, one day at a time.

A Parable

Observe
The faith of a caterpillar
That never questions "why."
Behold
What was a homely worm
Becomes a butterfly.

~ Mildred N. Hoyer
Daily Word

It is said that John Wesley was leading a discussion one day with a group of religious notables on the subject of faith. When asked to define the word faith, no one had a good answer. At last, a woman, overhearing this learned discussion, said, "It is taking God at his word."

"That will do," said Wesley. "It is enough for us all."

God's Handwriting

He writes in characters too grand
For our short sight to understand;
We catch but broken strokes, and try
To fathom all the mystery
Of withered hopes, of death, of life,
The endless war, the useless strife—
But there, with larger, clearer sight,
We shall see this—
    His way was right.

  ~ John Oxenham

A little girl went on her first visit to the dentist's office to have a tooth extracted. The dentist, realizing how scared the girl was, said: "Here, child, is a fifty-cent piece. You hold it in your hand, and after we are through you can have it." The little girl did not flinch through the operation. Afterward the dentist said, "You were so brave."

"Yes," she answered, "For the coin you gave me had inscribed on it, 'In God we Trust,' and that is what I did."

Letter from Abigail to John Adams

Braintree, Sunday, 16 September, 1775.

I set myself down to write with a heart depressed with the melancholy scenes around me. My letter will be only a bill of mortality; though thanks be to that Being who restraineth the pestilence, that it has not yet proved mortal to any of our family, though we live in daily expectation that Patty will not continue many hours. I had no idea of the distemper producing such a state as hers, till now. Two of the children, John and Charles, I have sent out of the house, finding it difficult to keep them out of the chamber. Tommy is better, but entirely stripped of the hardy, robust countenance, as well as of all the flesh he had, save what remains for to keep his bones together . . . Mrs. Randall has lost her daughter. Mrs. Bracket, hers. Mr. Thomas Thayer, his wife . . . I know of eight this week who have been buried in this town.

In Weymouth, it is very sickly, but not mortal. Dr. Tufts tells me he has between sixty and seventy patients now sick with this disorder . . . The dread upon the minds of people of catching the distemper is almost as great as if it was the small-pox.

We have been four Sundays without any meeting. Thus does pestilence travel in the rear of war, to remind us of our entire dependence upon that Being who not only directeth the arrow by day, but has also at his command that which flieth in darkness. So uncertain and so transitory are all the enjoyments of life, that were it not for the tender connections which bind us, would it not be folly to wish for continuance here? I think I shall never be wedded to the world, and were I to lose about a dozen of my dearest connections, I should have no further relish for life.

But perhaps I deceive myself and know little but little, of my own heart.

"To bear and suffer is our portion here."

And unto Him who mounts the whirlwind and directs the storm I will cheerfully leave the ordering of my lot, and whether adverse or prosperous days should be my future portion, I will trust in his right hand to lead me safely through, and, after a short rotation of events, fix me in a state immutable and happy . . .

God helps them that help themselves, as King Richard says; and if we can obtain the Divine aid by our own virtue, fortitude, and perseverance, we may be sure of relief.

To-morrow will be three weeks since you left home; in all which time I have not heard one word from you. Patience is a lesson I have not to learn, so I can wait your own time, but hope it will not be long ere my anxious heart is relieved . . . Oh, how I have longed for your bosom, to pour forth my sorrows there and find a healing balm; but perhaps that has been denied me that I might be led to a higher and a more permanent consolator who has bid us all call upon Him in the day of trouble.

Adieu! I need not say how sincerely I am
Your affectionate

～ Abigail Adams

In spite of everything, I still believe
that people are really good at heart.
I simply can't build up my hopes on a foundation
consisting of confusion, misery, and death.
I see the world gradually being turned into a wilderness.
I hear the ever-approaching thunder, which will
    destroy us, too,
I can feel the suffering of millions, and yet,
if I look up into the heavens,
I think that it will all come right,
that this cruelty will end,
And that peace and tranquility will return again.

～ Anne Frank

The day my husband was diagnosed with cancer, I was an emotional wreck. We spent the whole day getting second and third opinions regarding treatment options and came home exhausted at 5:00 P.M. A few minutes later, the doorbell rang and two good friends walked in with a complete dinner for our whole family. Yes, we could've ordered pizza that night, but there was something about chicken, mashed potatoes, and cherry pie that soothed our frazzled souls. I'll never forget that gesture of love.

JAMIE

This is our hope, this is the faith that I go back South with.

With this faith we will be able to hew out of the mountain of despair a stone of hope. With this faith we will be able to transform the jangling discords of our nation into a beautiful symphony of brotherhood.

With this faith we will be able to work together, to pray together, to struggle together, to go to jail together, to stand up for freedom together, knowing that we will be free one day.

Martin Luther King, Jr.
August 28, 1963

Nancy and Ed Huizinga in Grand Rapids, Michigan, know all about [suffering]. In December 1995, while they were at church rehearsing for the annual Christmas Festival of Lights program, their home burned to the ground. But that wasn't their only tragedy that year. Just three months earlier, Nancy's long-time friend, Barbara Post, a widow with two children, had died of cancer. Nancy and Ed had taken her two children, Jeff and Katie, into their home as part of their family, something they had promised Barb they would do. So when Ed and Nancy's house burned to the ground just before Christmas, it wasn't just their home that was lost; it was the home of two teenagers who had already lost their mother and father.

As circumstances unfolded, irony went to work. The tragedy that forced the Huizingas from their home allowed Jeff and Katie to move back to theirs. Since their home had not yet been sold following their mother's death, they and the Huizinga family moved in there the night after the fire.

On the following Saturday, neighbors organized a party to sift through the ashes and search for anything of value that might have survived. One of the first indications they received of God's involvement in their struggle came as a result of that search. Somehow a piece of paper survived. On it were the words: "Contentment: Realizing that God has already provided everything we need for our present happiness."

To Nancy and Ed, this was like hearing God speak from a burning bush. It was the assurance they needed that He was there . . . and He was not silent.

~ Charles R. Swindoll
   Hope Again

God is very powerful. He made the whole world in six days. It takes me that long to clean my room.

~ Sarah Roark, age 11

God makes us head-first and then He adds body and legs. And last He reaches inside his own body and puts some soul in us. And He gives us guts. His guts.

~ Jack Finlay, age 6

Lord, I have been so defeated by circumstances. I have felt like an animal trapped in a corner with nowhere to flee. Where are you in all this, Lord? The night is dark. I cannot feel Your presence.

Help me to know that the darkness is really "shade of Your hand, outstretched caressingly"; that the "hemming in" is Your doing. Perhaps there was no other way You could get my full attention, no other way I would allow You to demonstrate what You can do in my life.

I see now that the emptier my cup is, the more space there is to receive Your love and supply.

～ Catherine Marshall
Adventures in Prayer

God is like a shepherd. He watches over us and makes sure we don't fall off the edge.

～ Emily Landis, age 9

On the one-year anniversary of the delivery of my stillborn baby girl, a dozen pink baby roses were delivered to my home. They were from a sweet friend who knew how much I was still hurting. It was nice just to know someone was thinking of me and recognized that the pain lingers even years later.

∽ PRISCILLA

Happiness is not a state to arrive at, but a manner of traveling.

∽ Margaret Lee Runbeck

Hope is better conveyed by the Spanish word "esperanza" which translates as hope coupled with expectation. It provides an anticipated sureness that the clouds will lift or people will rise above them.

∽ Candy S. Krausman

Two little children were put early to bed on a winter's night, for the fire had gone out, and the cold was pouring in at the many cracks of their frail shanty.

The mother strove to eke out the scantiness of the bed-covering by placing clean boards over the children. A pair of bright eyes shone out from under a board, and just before it was hushed in slumber, a sweet voice said, "Mother, how nice this is! How I pity the poor people who don't have any boards to cover their children with this cold night."

Help me to see that although
I am in the wilderness
It is not all briars and barrenness.
I have bread from heaven,
Streams from the rock.
Light by day, fire by night,
Thy dwelling place and thy mercy seat.
I am sometimes discouraged by the way,
But though winding and trying,
It is safe and short.

~ Puritan Prayer
The Valley of Vision

My father was suffering through the end of a long struggle with bone cancer. He still weighed enough and was in such pain that it was hard work to move him from a chair to his bed. Others far more heroic than I spent the months and the days caring for him. But I took some turns on the midnight to dawn shift.

The effects of disease had removed the powers of reason he'd used to make the mark that is still visible in science. He seemed to me almost like a child as we talked through the night. Most of his memories were of riding across the range together with his father in Old Mexico. But sometimes even those happy pictures could not crowd from his mind the terrible pain.

One night when I was not with him and the pain seemed more than he could bear, he somehow got out of bed and on his knees beside it—I know not how. He pled with God to know why he was suffering so. And the next morning he said to me, with quiet firmness, "I know why now. God needs brave sons."

During his lifetime, my father had gone from Berkeley to Berlin and on to Princeton and had created theories that changed the scientific world. But what he learned on his knees that night is what brought him peace.

~ Henry B. Eyring
   To Draw Closer to God

A Soldier—His Prayer

Stay with me, God. The night is dark,
The night is cold: my little spark
Of courage dies. The night is long;
Be with me, God, and make me strong.

I love a game; I love a fight.
I hate the dark; I love the light.
I love my child; I love my wife.
I am no coward. I love Life.

Life with its change of mood and shade.
I want to live. I'm not afraid.
But me and mine are hard to part;
Oh, unknown God, lift up my heart.

You stilled the waters at Dunkirk
And saved Your Servants. All Your work
Is wonderful, dear God. You strode
Before us down that dreadful road.

We were alone, and hope had fled;
We loved our country and our dead,
And could not shame them; so we stayed
The course, and were not much afraid.

Dear God that nightmare road! And then
That sea! We got there—we were men.
My eyes were blind, my feet were torn,
My soul sang like a bird at dawn!

I knew that death is but a door.
I knew what we were fighting for:
Peace for the kids, our brothers freed,
A kinder world, a cleaner breed.

I'm but the son my mother bore,
A simple man, and nothing more.
But—God of strength and gentleness,
Be pleased to make me nothing less.

Help me, O God, when Death is near
To mock the haggard face of fear,
That when I fall—if fall I must—
My soul may triumph in the Dust.

⟳ Anonymous
    (This poem was blown into a slit trench in Tunisia during a heavy
    bombardment in the early days of World War II.)

⟳

175

I Won't Give Up on Him

I recently heard about a father who was working outside his home when he noticed his 5-year-old daughter sprawled on the driveway, completely focused on the cement in front of her.

Curious, he strolled up behind her to see what was so mesmerizing. There on the driveway a caterpillar was making its way across what, for it, was a vast expanse, fraught with obstacles and danger. The girl was absolutely spellbound, watching as the creature's tiny legs and body propelled its slinky way to . . . well, wherever it was going.

"Caterpillars sure are interesting, aren't they?" the father said at last.

The little girl didn't take her eyes off the driveway. She just grunted, "Uh-huh."

"It looks like it would take a lot of work to move like that, doesn't it?" Dad asked.

"Uh-huh."

He understood. He remembered the fascination of watching creeping things crawl as a boy. They quietly watched for a few minutes, as the caterpillar struggled to negotiate a wide crack in the pavement. "Before too long," the father noted, "he won't have to worry about big cracks like that."

"Why not?" the girl wondered.

"He'll just fly over the top of it," Dad said.

For the first time, the little girl looked up. "Nah-ahhhh," she said. "Caterpillars don't fly."

"You're right—they don't," Dad replied. "But they turn into butterflies, and you've seen how well butterflies can fly.

"It's the truth," Dad said. "You can ask Mom. One of these days this caterpillar will build a little home for itself called a cocoon, and then he'll go to sleep for awhile. When he wakes up he'll crawl out of his cocoon, only by then he will have turned into a butterfly, and he'll fly away."

His daughter was suspicious. "Daddy, is this sort of like that tooth fairy story?"

"No, sweetheart," he replied, "This is true. It's really going to happen. Honest."

"Well, OK," she said. Then she smiled and turned her attention back to the caterpillar. "I was worried about him," she said. "But if he's really going to be able to fly, I won't give up on him."

All of us find ourselves occasionally limited by mortality. Sometimes we're forced by circumstances to move slowly, struggling to overcome each new obstacle in our way. At other times we encounter limitations that are even more restrictive, binding us in a cocoon of disability, depression or hardship. At such times the easiest solution would be to simply give up. And while I understand why some choose to do exactly that, I am in awe of those who refuse to surrender to life's vicissitudes. Like the caterpillar that emerges from its confining chrysalis to spread its wings as a beautiful butterfly, they burst free of the constraints mortality imposes upon them. And they fly.

In a world where earth-bound caterpillars end up soaring with the birds, you learn not to give up on anyone who hasn't already given up on themselves.

～ Joseph B. Walker

When you get into a tight place and everything goes against you, till it seems as though you could not hang on a minute longer, never give up then, for that is just the place and time that the tide will turn.

～ Harriet Beecher Stowe

Courage is the price that life exacts for granting peace. The soul that knows it not, knows no release from little things.

～ Amelia Earhart

God of our life,
there are days when the burdens we carry
chafe our shoulders and weigh us down;
when the road seems dreary and endless,
the skies gray and threatening;
when our lives have no music in them,
and our hearts are lonely,
and our souls have lost their courage.
Flood the path with light,
run our eyes to where
the skies are full of promise;
tune our hearts to brave music;
give us the sense of comradeship
with heroes and saints of every age;
and so quicken our spirits
that we may be able to encourage
the souls of all who journey with us
on the road of life, to your honor and glory.

～ St. Augustine

Courage is armor
A blind man wears;
The calloused scar
Of outlived despairs:
Courage is Fear
That has said its prayers.

~ Karle Wilson Baker

What keeps our faith cheerful is the extreme persistence of
gentleness and humor. Gentleness is everywhere in daily
life, a sign that faith rules through ordinary things: through
cooking and small talk, through storytelling, making love,
fishing, tending animals and sweet corn and flowers,
through sports, music, and books, raising kids—all the
places where the gravy soaks in and grace shines through.
Even in a time of elephantine vanity and greed, one never
has to look far to see the campfires of gentle people.
Lacking any other purpose in life, it would be good
enough to live for their sake.

~ Garrison Keillor

Forgive, O Lord, my little jokes
    on Thee
And I'll forgive Thy great big one
    on me.

~∽ Robert Frost
    In the Clearing

One has to abandon altogether the search for security,
and reach out to the risk of living with both arms.
One has to embrace the world like a lover.
One has to accept pain as a condition of existence.
One has to court doubt and darkness as the cost
    of knowing.
One needs a will stubborn in conflict, but apt always
    to total acceptance of every consequence of living
    and dying.

~∽ Morris L. West

There is in every person's heart a spark of heavenly fire which lies dormant in the broad daylight of prosperity, but which kindles up and beams and blazes in the dark hour of adversity.

~ Washington Irving

We never know how high we are
Till we are called to rise
And then if we are true to plan
Our statures touch the skies.

~ Emily Dickinson

The world is round and the place which may seem like the end may also be the beginning.

~ Ivy Baker Priest

183

ACKNOWLEDGMENTS

THE AUTHOR GRATEFULLY ACKNOWLEDGES PERMISSION TO
reprint from the following works: *Fresh Crab and French
Bread* by Garnee Falkner, Copyright © 1985 by Intellectual
Reserve, Inc. *The Traveling Smile* by Jane Bunker Newcomb,
Copyright © 1985 by Intellectual Reserve, Inc. *Dandelions*
by Penny Allen, Copyright © 1978 by Intellectual Reserve,
Inc. *Raymond and the Bus* by Kathleen Conger Ellis,
Copyright © 1981 by Intellectual Reserve, Inc. *God is No
Illusion* by John Tully Carmody, Copyright © 1997, Trinity
Press International. *The Road Less Traveled* by M. Scott Peck,
M.D. reprinted by permission of Simon & Schuster Adult
Publishing Group, Copyright © 1978 by M. Scott Peck, M.D.